FACING LIFE AND GETTING THE BEST OF IT

FACING LIFE AND GETTING THE BEST OF IT

By

CLARENCE EDWARD MACARTNEY

MINISTER, FIRST PRESBYTERIAN CHURCH, PITTSBURGH, PA.

ABINGDON-COKESBURY PRESS
NEW YORK • NASHVILLE

FACING LIFE AND GETTING THE
BEST OF IT
COPYRIGHT, MCMXL
BY WHITMORE & SMITH

E

FOREWORD

As originally planned, this series of sermons, FACING LIFE AND GETTING THE BEST OF IT, was made up of seven sermons; but the reactions to these seven sermons as I preached them from Sunday night to Sunday night prompted me to expand the series, until it now numbers fourteen sermons.

For some time I had been turning over in my mind the thought which often comes, I am sure, to all ministers, and to all earnest Christians, too, how to make a little plainer and clearer the application of Christian truths to our daily life. The result of those meditations and desires was this series of sermons on FACING LIFE AND GETTING THE BEST OF IT. The different situations which confront our soul on this our earthly pilgrimage and warfare are manifold; yet I feel that many of the major problems, difficulties, and temptations of life are dealt with in these fourteen sermons.

We must all face life. How shall we face it? Will life get the best of us, or shall we get the best of it? Man is either master over life, or he is mastered by life. He either gets the mastery over the passions and sorrows, the wounds and the disappointments, the fears and transgressions of life, or they get the mastery over him.

The last time I was in London, two years ago, I came upon the saying of a famous English psychologist. After years of experience in dealing with the ills and troubles and sins and passions of men and women, he goes on record as saying, "There is no victory in life save through religion."

Whatever the fault of these sermons, no one can say that they do not touch life, life which has such solemn possibilities of evil, and yet is so radiant with possibilities of beauty and good and power. Christ came that we might have life, and that we might have it more abundantly.

In these sermons on FACING LIFE AND GETTING THE BEST OF IT I have endeavored to show, on the ground of the inspired teachings of the Bible, and as illustrated in the life of Christ, and in the lives of His friends and disciples, how it is possible for all to get the victory over life, through faith, which overcometh the world.   CLARENCE EDWARD MACARTNEY

CONTENTS

I

GETTING THE BEST OF FEAR

"Fear not"
Genesis 15:1; Revelation 1:17

"FEAR not." God says that more times than anything else in the Bible. From Genesis to Revelation, from Abraham to John on Patmos, we hear that command, appeal, and exhortation. It is spoken by the mouth of prophets, apostles, martyrs, and by Christ Himself. "Fear not." To Abraham, to Israel, to Moses, to David, to Daniel, to Jerusalem, to the Disciples, to the women at the sepulcher, to Zacharias, to Mary the mother of our Lord, to Simon, to Jairus, to Paul, to John, and to many others under all kinds of conditions and circumstances, that is the word we hear God speak to those who believe in Him: "Fear not."

The frequency with which the Bible tells us not to fear agrees with the fact that fear is the great spoiler and enemy of man's life.

I

THE RAVAGES OF FEAR

Fear is man's greatest adversary. According to an ancient legend, a man driving one day to Constantinople was stopped by an old woman who asked him for a ride. He took her up beside him and, as they drove along, he looked at her and became frightened and asked, "Who are you?"

The old woman replied: "I am Cholera."

Thereupon the peasant ordered the old woman to get down and walk; but she persuaded him to take her along upon her promise that she would not kill more than five people in Constantinople. As a pledge of the promise she handed him a dagger, saying to him that it was the only weapon with which she could be killed. Then she added: "I shall meet you in two days. If I break my promise, you may stab me."

In Constantinople one hundred and twenty people died of the cholera. The enraged man who had driven her to the city, and to whom she had given the dagger as a pledge that she would not kill more than five, went out to look for the old woman, and meeting her, raised his dagger to kill her. But she stopped him, saying: "I have kept my agreement. I killed only five. Fear killed the others."

This legend is a true parable of life. Where disease kills its thousands, fear kills its tens of thousands. The greatest miseries of mankind come from the dread of trouble rather than from the presence of trouble. From the cradle to the grave fear casts its baleful shadow. Fear betrays man's spirit, breaks down his defense, disarms him in the battle, unfits him for the work of life, and adds terror to the dying bed.

Fear is the most universal instinct, and, according to the biologists, the oldest of human instincts. It must be an instinct which, although useful for the preservation of man's life, is due to the presence of sin in the world, for the beautiful Scriptural fore-casts of the Messianic age show us a world from which fear has been banished. "There is none to molest or make afraid," and the little child walks between the leopard and the lion. Fear in the form of worry is the greatest, most harmful, most senseless, most useless, and most universal of all sins. Like the sword of Damocles, fear hangs with its threat over the head of man.

II

THE DIFFERENT KINDS OF FEAR

It would take a long catalogue to exhaust the vari-ous kinds of fear. Some who are well are afraid they will get sick; some who are sick are afraid they will not get well; some who are young are afraid of old age coming on. Some who have beauty are afraid of the day when beauty has vanished. Others are afraid of unemployment, or the loss of money, or injury to their good name, or the sickness or death of those whom they love. Men are not always sick, or sad, or lonely, or suffering, but a great many all the time are afraid of these things. In his ode "To a Skylark," Shelley says truthfully:

> "We look before and after
>   And pine for what is not;
> Our sincerest laughter
>   With some pain is fraught."

In one of the great scenes in Goethe's "Faust," four gray sisters appear at midnight at the palace door. These are Want, Guilt, Necessity, and Care. The first three are unable to enter the palace, but the keyhole is free to the entrance of Care. When Faust addressed Care after it had entered the palace, Care responded:

> "Though no ear should choose to hear me,
>   Yet the shrinking heart must fear me;
> Though transformed to mortal eyes,
> Grimmest powers I exercise.
> On the land or ocean, yonder,
> I, a dread companion, wander,
> Always found, yet never sought.
>
> Whom I once possess shall never
> Find the world worth his endeavour;
> Endless gloom around him folding,
> Rise nor set of sun beholding,
> And he knows not how to measure
> True possession of his treasure.
> Be it happiness or sorrow,
> He postpones it till the morrow;
> To the future only cleaveth—
> Nothing, therefore, he achieveth."

That is a true description of the effects of care. It weakens men, saddens them, frightens them, and blinds them to the satisfactions of life. Regardless of what men's profession of faith may be, if they are under the dominion of fear, they are practical atheists, "for God hath not given us the spirit of fear; but of love, and of a sound mind." It would be interesting to take your stand in the street pulpit in front of this church and look down upon the procession of humanity as it passes. Did you possess the magic power to look beneath the surface of their breast and see what is really in their heart, you would be surprised to learn the great number and variety of fears to which man is subject, from the fear of a child as it comes into this world, to the man's fear of life's last experience, which is death. And what could be sadder than this, when we consider what man is, created in the image of God, made for dominion over the world, with the intellect of an angel, and with an immortal soul, and yet the victim and slave of a thousand fears.

Fear was the first wages of sin; for when the man and the woman yielded to the tempter and ate of the forbidden fruit, we read that "they heard the voice of the Lord God walking in the garden at the cool of the day, and they hid themselves from the presence of the Lord God amongst the trees of the garden"; and when God called unto Adam and said unto him,

"Where art thou?" he said, "I heard Thy voice in the garden, and I was afraid." That was the first shadow cast by fear over the world, and ever since fear has been blighting and darkening the life of man.

III

THE CURE AND REMEDY FOR FEAR

Some one has said that the greatest blessing which one could bestow upon mankind, the greatest contribution which one could make for the well-being of mankind, would be to devise some way to banish fear from man's life. The great remedy, the only complete remedy, of course, is what the Bible offers us, trust and confidence in God, and the casting of all our care upon Him. But there are a number of considerations which ought to help those who are the victims of fear.

One of these is the obvious fact that a large per cent of the things which we dread never happen. Probably, if a man could keep a register of his fears through twenty-five or fifty years of life, it would show that a very small percentage of the things which he dreaded came to pass. In his house in Chelsea in London they show you the sound-proof chamber, a sort of vaulted apartment, which Carlyle had built in his house so that all the noise of the street would be shut out and he could do his work in unbroken silence. One of his neighbors, however, kept a cock that several times in the night and in the early morning gave way to vigorus self-expression. When Carlyle protested to the owner of the cock, the man pointed out to him that the cock crowed only three times in the night, and that after all that could not be such a terrible annoyance. "But," Carlyle said to him, "if you only knew what I suffer waiting for that cock to crow!" There are a lot of people like that in life, harassed and suffering, because they are waiting for something disastrous and unpleasant to happen.

Another helpful consideration is that even the heaviest troubles will pass away. That was what Lincoln used to say to himself so often in the midst of his many distresses, "This, too, shall pass away." That was the word that an Eastern king had written on a ring given him by his daughter. Unable to control his anxious moments, he asked his wise men in vain for a cure. Then his daughter gave him a ring with this inscription upon it, "This, too, shall pass away"; and the monarch's fears subsided. Theodore Tilton, in his poem "Even This Shall Pass Away," says on this subject:

> "Once in Persia reigned a king
> Who upon his signet ring
> Graved a maxim true and wise,
> Which, if held before the eyes,
> Gave him wisdom at a glance,
> Fit for every change and chance.

Solemn words and these are they:
'Even this shall pass away'!"

In a book written by an American diplomat who recently retired from long service, I found this illuminating sentence, where he refers to some difficulty and trouble that he had, "And like all others, it marched on."

There is a great deal, too, in the power of will when it comes to dealing with our fears. If a man will not be mastered by his fears, he will be able to conquer them. An officer going once into battle, and seeing his legs shaking with fear, thus addressed his legs: "Legs, you are shaking now; but what would you do if you knew where I am going to take you today?"

Common sense, too, if applied to many of the fears of life, would make them vanish. George Herbert said that if you see a ghost in a field at night, go up and speak to him, and you will generally find that the ghost is nothing but a sheet hung out to dry.

It is important, too, to remember that fear and worry are useless. Whether things that we dread come to pass or not, our fearing them in advance can in no respect hold them back, or diminish their power. Nothing is so useless as fear. That is what Christ emphasizes about the folly of worry. I think there is almost humor in what He says on that subject. "Which of you," He says, "by taking thought can add one cubit to his stature?" That is what He says on the subject of taking anxious thought about the future. "Sufficient unto the day is the evil thereof." You cannot cross the bridge before you come to it.

The greatest cure of all for fear is trust in the care and providence of God. We talk about that, and we sing about it, and yet how much do we really practice it? That is a great verse in the Psalms, "Ye that fear the Lord trust in him." If we believe in the Lord, let us put our trust in Him. Lincoln used to tell a story of a woman who had been in a runaway and said she trusted in Providence until the breeching broke. During a storm at sea, when it seemed that the vessel might go down, a distraught woman went to the captain and asked him what the prospects were. "Madam," said the captain, "we must trust in Providence." "Oh," exclaimed the woman, throwing up her hands in despair, "has it come to that!"

God answers and delivers us, not so much by removing the evil or the danger, but by showing us His face, by walking by our side. That's what He did with Paul. Paul three times earnestly besought God to pluck the thorn out of his flesh, that mysterious affliction, that messenger of Satan which so tormented him and humiliated him. But the answer of Christ was, "My grace is sufficient for thee: for my strength is made perfect in weakness." When we are troubled and harrassed by fear, let us remember how many times in the past, when things that we had dreaded at length came, we were given a strength to meet them and bear them.

So strength comes to us equal to our desire. "As thy days, so shall thy strength be." How many promises of God's Word there are which are of a nature to deliver us from fear! They are like moles, or sea walls, thrust out into the deep, and within their shelter all is peace and quiet. Dwight L. Moody's favorite verse was Isaiah 12:2, "I will trust, and not be afraid." He used to say, "You can travel first class or second class to heaven. Second class is, 'What time I am afraid, I will trust.' First class is, 'I will trust and not be afraid.'" That is the better way. Why not buy a first-class ticket?

Forever true is that great scene of our Lord and His disciples in the boat in the storm at sea. When they thought that the boat was going to sink, they went to Him where He was sleeping on a cushion on the stern of the boat and awakening Him cried, "Master, carest Thou not that we perish?" Jesus stilled the tempest and stilled their fears. But He also gave them a sermon which they never forgot, and which is timely and practical for us tonight. It was this: "O ye of little faith!"

As Bacon put it in his celebrated essay, "Men fear death as children fear to go in the dark." My own experience at many deathbeds has been to the effect that death is its own anesthetist and banishes fear in the mind of the dying. But because so many dread that last experience in life, it will be always true that cowards die many times. The Christian, last of all men, should fear death. On a dark afternoon in September, 1583, and in a stormy sea, near the Azores, the *Golden Hind*, commanded by Sir Walter Raleigh, sailed close to the *Squirrel*, a smaller vessel commanded by Sir Humphrey Gilbert. Sailing close to the *Squirrel*, the captain of the *Golden Hind* cried out to Gilbert, who was sitting in the stern of his vessel with a book open in his hand, and urged him for his safety to come aboard the larger vessel. This Gilbert refused to do, saying he would not leave his companions in the *Squirrel*. Then the captain of the *Golden Hind* heard him call out over the waves, "Heaven is as near by sea as by land." At midnight that night those on the *Golden Hind* saw the lights on the smaller vessel suddenly go out, and in that moment Gilbert and his ship were swallowed up by the dark and raging sea.

Heaven is as near by sea as by land! That was a true Christian sentiment. That was what Paul meant in that great sentence of his, "Whether we live or whether we die, we are the Lord's." Live in that faith, and fear will no longer have dominion over you. And this will be the victory that overcometh the world, even your faith.

GETTING THE BEST OF LOVE AND SEX

"Set me as a seal upon thine heart, as a seal upon thine arm: for love is strong as death; jealousy is cruel as the grave; the coals thereof are coals of fire, which hath a most vehement flame. Many waters cannot quench love, neither can the floods drown it; if a man would give all the substance of his house for love, it would utterly be contemned"
Song of Solomon 8:6, 7

THESE words of the Song of Solomon are perhaps the noblest love lyric ever written or sung. Here you have set forth the strength, the origin, the unquenchableness, and the sanctity of true love. A great critic, Saintsbury, declared it was the finest love lyric in our language.

In this series, FACING LIFE AND HOW TO GET THE BEST OF IT, we deal with those things which are so powerful that they sometimes get the best of men and women. If this were not so, there would be no significance in this general topic, FACING LIFE AND GETTING THE BEST OF IT. In the last chapter we spoke of man's Enemy Number One, FEAR, and the

[21]

shadow that fear casts over man's life. Our present topic is LOVE. Love lifts men to thrones of influence and crowns them with diadems of happiness. But where it is abused, sinned against, and defiled, there it degrades man and enslaves him.

No one can face life without facing the fact of this great emotion. Perhaps one would not exaggerate, if one were to say that love is the greatest factor in human happiness and also the greatest source of unhappiness. The importance and power of love lies in the fact that it represents one of the three elemental hungers in man's nature, which are said to be, the hunger for food, the hunger of sex and love, and the desire for property. Whoever faces life must face this emotion; and this by virtue of our creation, for "male and female created He them."

> "Still slowly passed the melancholy day
> And still the stranger wist not where to stray;
> The world was sad, the garden was a wild,
> And man, the hermit, sighed till woman smiled."

According to the legend of Pandora and her box, only Hope was left when she succeeded in getting the cover back on the box again. The one thing that man saved out of the wreck of Eden was love. Once there hung before a haunted castle an enchanted harp, with this legend enscrolled on its rim of gold:

> "Whatever bard would win me
> Must strike and wake within me,
> By one supreme endeavor,
> A chord that sounds forever."

By command of the king three bards were summoned to the trial to find and strike this magic chord. As the bards played, throngs of knights and ladies watched and listened. The first bard, a hoary old minstrel, sang loudly of war and its glory, and of battles fought and won. His music evoked much applause; yet, in spite of this praise, the magic harp ceased its vibration. Then the second bard came forward. Instead of fire and sword and battle, he sang a song of pleasure, of drinking and toasting, and as he sang and played the walls of the castle resounded with merry laughter; but soon the harp again was silent.

Then came forward the third bard, and with his soul on fire he sang of the pure passion of love. As he smote the wire the enthralled listeners caught up a wreath and crowned him:

> "That crown hath faded never,
> That harp resounds forever."

It is with that ever-resounding harp and chord of love that we deal with here.

I

THOSE WHO ARE MASTERED BY LOVE AND SEX

We shall speak first of those who are mastered by

love and sex, mastered to their own hurt and sorrow, and sometimes to their shame and degradation. Love sinned against and abused is a terrible master. This elemental emotion in man's nature, given an abnormal place, becomes a persecutor and tormentor. This has always been a danger; but that danger is vastly increased today. In popular books, in plays and in films, in songs of crooners over the radio, and even in the business advertisements, love and sex are exploited for gain or popularity. The effect of all this is to push the idea of sex on the youth of today as never before in the history of mankind.

The world is strewn with the wreckage of lives in which this God-given instinct has been defiled and abused and turned aside from its high and proper and noble purpose. There is no devastation like this. There is nothing that so hardens, corrupts, corrodes, blasts and blights, debases and degrades man, as uncontrolled love, without honor and without God. In the history of Sampson in the Bible we have an example of the degrading and unmanning influence of unhallowed love and unhallowed marriage. In the story of the Gadarene, out of whom Christ cast the legion of devils, the devils besought Jesus that He would "send them into the swine." Whoever abuses and dishonors the love instinct in his life is, in effect, making a prayer that he be sent into the swine, for nothing brings man down to the level of the swine, and far below it, so quickly as uncontrolled and unhallowed love. When Ulysses was on his famous voyage he and his men landed at the island where Circe lived. When they came into her court, Circe touched the seamen of Ulysses and immediately they were transformed into swine—bristles, snout, hoofs, and all—but with the intellect of a man. Sad and terrible, but a true parable of how the touch of the wand of lust turns men into swine.

II
THE PATH TO CONQUEST. HOW SHALL ONE GET THE VICTORY

Plato used to describe man's nature under the figure of two horses, a black horse and a white horse; and happiness and success in life depend upon how man drives those two horses, or the relationship of his physical to his mental and spiritual life. It is possible for man to rise to the dignity of self-control, because God has made him a little lower than the angels. He has physical instincts, but also moral and spiritual. He has a living soul, and precisely because he is more than a brute he can exercise self-control and "keep the body under."

One of the secrets of self-control is to have a deep reverence for our own person. It was a "just and pious reverence for my own person," Milton said, which kept him from the transgressions which disgraced the lives of his fellow students at Cambridge.

Another aid in the conquest of this elemental emotion and in keeping it in its true place and preserving it for its honorable uses, is wholesome thoughts and occupations. When Ulysses came near the sirens on his wanderings and his ship was likely to be drawn into the whirlpool, he had himself and his fellow sailors bound to the mast so that they might resist the bewitching music. But on another occasion they had Orpheus play his lyre, and that sweet music made the mariners deaf to the beguiling and seducing music of the sirens. The lower music of life has little effect upon us when we are listening to the higher music of life. Especially on the part of men, high and worthy thoughts of women are a safeguard. Over one of the halls frequented by soldiers in Paris is this inscription: "When you think of women, think of your mother, your sister, your sweetheart, your wife, and you will not think bestially."

Another important aid in self-control is the avoidance of places, books, plays, and persons which abnormally turn the mind to this relationship in life. And how many such places, plays, books, films, and even persons there are to be avoided!

Another help is right friendships. I received a letter recently from a friend in the South asking me to look up a young man who had come to the city. In his account of the young man, speaking of his Christian faith and training and general characteristics, he said, "He is careful in the choice of his friends." That is one of the most important safeguards for young men and young women, to be careful in the choice of their friends. In the narrative of one of the darkest and most shameful tragedies in the Bible, it is said of the chief actor in that tragedy, "He had a friend." But he was the wrong kind of a friend.

Most important of all aids to self-mastery and self-control is religious faith and practice. It is not without significance that the Bible, and especially the New Testament, speaks so frequently, and so very plainly, on the subject of this sermon. In the warnings and exhortations which the Bible gives, the thing which is emphasized as man's safeguard and defense is the fear of God and the love of Christ. It is this which arms man against the degradation of himself. Mere knowledge as to the dire results of the abuse of love, or the degradation and punishment which ensue, is not enough. There must be a positive religious principle. In *The Temptation of St. Anthony*, by Flaubert, when the unclean and licentious temptresses swarmed about him in his cave, and he was about to yield, the face of Christ appeared unto him and the unclean tormentors disappeared.

III

VICTORY OVER BITTER EXPERIENCES OR DISAPPOINTMENTS IN THIS FIELD OF HUMAN RELATIONSHIP

There is an altogether different type of experience which must not be neglected or forgotten in any complete treatment of this subject. I mean the unhappy or bitter experience or disappointment which not a few have had in human relationships. Some were disappointed before marriage! some disappointed in marriage. Now the question arises, How are they going to face such an experience? Will they master it, or will it master them?

Some of the most beautiful chapters in human achievement have been written by those who rose above their sorrow, or disappointment, or bitter experience, and turned the whole stream of their affection into a channel of good will and service to mankind. One of the most gifted men ever to sit in the United States Senate was the famous Charles Sumner, a great figure there before, during, and after the Civil War. Commenting on the assault made upon him by Preston S. Brooks in the Senate in 1851, Sumner said: "When I was assaulted in the Senate Chamber in 1851, no one thought I would live. In the weary months of illness that followed, my thoughts were much on my unfinished fight against slavery. But in the midnight watches my keenest heart-gnawing regret was that if I were called away I never had enjoyed the choicest experience of life, that no lips responsive to my own had said, 'I love you.'" In 1866 Sumner was married to Mrs. Alice Hooper, and full of radiant hopes for the future. But all these hopes were dashed, for his family life was embittered, his love for his wife turned into hatred, and his hopes of handing his name to posterity into unforgiving anger. One would not say that Sumner was mastered by this unfortunate experience in his life, for even after it he continued to render distinguished service to his country; but his greatest work had been done before this bitterness came into his life. It added nothing to his usefulness and his influence.

But there have been not a few who, unfortunate in marriage, or disappointed in love, only gave more freely of their spirit and personality for the good of mankind. One of the gifted sisters of Henry Ward Beecher was Catherine Beecher. She was engaged to be married to the brilliant prodigy, Alexander Metcalf Fisher, of Yale College, who was drowned in the wreck of a ship off the Irish coast. This almost shattered her life; but recovering from the blow, she determined, as she put it, to "find happiness in living to do good." And that, after all, is the great end and purpose of life and that is the only kind of happiness that abides.

Marriage, which is the fulfillment and culmination of love, is a blessing or a burden, according to whether or not it is a marriage with the love and fear of God in it. Where the love of God is lacking, there we have all the elements of shipwreck and misery. Among the orthodox Jews, when a man and a woman are married a glass is placed before the bridegroom, who breaks it with his foot. This signifies that if the fear of God is in the hearts of the married, there will be peace and love; but if not, it means fire and flame. This is an ancient symbolism which finds repeated and striking fulfillment in many a marriage today. Without God, you have marriages and relationships like that of Samson and the women who deceived him and betrayed him. With God, you have marriages like Jacob and Rachel which bless and comfort and inspire to the very end.

There died recently in Brooklyn a woman over ninety years of age, and when she was laid away in her grave on her finger was the ring of engagement which had been given to her by her lover, a Captain Seth. Before their marriage could he consummated, the Civil War broke out and he went off to war, where he gave the last full measure of his devotion. Through all these seventy-nine years, this woman wore the ring as the symbol of their plighted love and the hope of their reunion in another world. That is the kind of love the woman who speaks in the Song of Songs was thinking of when she said, "Set me as a seal upon thine heart, as a seal upon thine arm: for love is strong as death. Many waters cannot quench love, neither can the floods drown it: if a man would give all the substance of his house for love, it would utterly be contemned." That kind of love is sacred! There is no substitute for it, nothing that can represent its value. All the substance of the world could not buy it.

At the same time, let it be remembered that there is great usefulness and great beauty in life altogether outside of this realm of personal affection between man and woman. Some of the noblest benefactors of mankind have apparently been strangers to this emotion, and no one ought to conclude that the lack of this experience in any way disqualifies one for the highest ministry or the highest place in life. There is no doubt, however, that, for the generality of the people, the deepest satisfaction and the deepest usefulness will be found in marriage. The ancient declaration made at the beginning of man's existence still holds, "It is not good that man should be alone."

> "Somewhere there waiteth in this world of ours
>   For one lone soul another lonely soul,
> Each choosing each through all the weary hours,
>   And meeting strangely, at one sudden goal,
> Then blend they, like green leaves with golden flowers,
>   Into one beautiful and perfect whole;

And life's long night is ended, and the way
  Lies open onward to eternal day." [1]

Whether it be single life, or marriage, or study, or
art, or music, or business, what transfigures it and
purifies it and sanctifies it is the friendship of Jesus
Christ; and that friendship I now gladly and earnestly commend unto you.

[1] Edwin Arnold.

III

GETTING THE BEST OF TEMPTATION

"And when the tempter came—"

Matthew 4:3

HE is sure to come, and when he comes, then a critical hour has struck for the soul. Then everything—innocence, hope, joy, and strength—depends not upon what the tempter does, but upon what the tempted does. The recording angel waits with uplifted pen to write and put on record what the tempted soul has done.

Always the tempter is coming. He misses no individual, skips no race or age. Ever since the fall he has been coming. Seedtime and harvest, summer and winter, heat and cold, never fail to come; neither does temptation. That desert scene in the life of our Lord is timeless and universal, for temptation is as eternal as human history and as universal as human nature.

The temptation of our Lord took place at the beginning of His ministry. Before He began to preach He was driven into the wilderness to be tempted of the devil. All His work as a Redeemer depended upon what Christ did in that moment when the tempter came. So the usefulness and strength and honor of life may depend upon what a soul does in the moment of temptation, and whether it gets the best of temptation, or temptation gets the best of the soul.

The Bible has no high-sounding theories or hypotheses as to the source and origin of evil and temptation. It declares plainly that the tempter, the originator of evil in man, is Satan or the Devil, who is the great adversary of man's soul. If Christ was not too great to be tempted of the devil, neither are you and I. The devil is often voted not to be today; but someone certainly is doing his work, sowing tares where the wheat has been sown, mixing the fatal draught that palsies the heart and brain of man, dogging the steps of the toiling saints and digging pits for his feet, blighting the land with his fiery breath. A French priest was once addressed by a young man who said to him, "I suppose you no longer believe in a devil?" "Yes," said the priest, "I do; for if I did not believe in the devil, I would have to believe that I was my own devil." This fact, taught by Christ and the Bible, that man is the object of a hostile interest on the part of the Prince of Evil himself, adds to the solemnity of our subject, for it lets us know that man is assailed not only by evil motives and desires, but by the great spirit of evil himself, who goes about seeking whom he may devour. In the literal translation, the Lord's Prayer reads, not, "Lead us not into temptation, but deliver us from evil," but "Lead us not into temptation, but deliver us from the *Evil One.*"

In taking up this great and solemn theme of temptation, we shall speak first of some of the different kinds of temptation, and then of our armor and our defense against them.

I

THE DIFFERENT KINDS OF TEMPTATION

Here we can follow, to a certain extent, the history of the temptation of our Lord; for although He was God manifest in the flesh, He was also made in all things like unto His brethren and was tempted like as we are.

The first temptation of Jesus was a temptation of the flesh. The devil came to Him after He had fasted forty days and forty nights "and was a hungered." It was then that he suggested to Him that if He was the Son of God, He should turn the stones of the desert into bread that He might eat. That would have been no temptation to one who was not hungry, but after a fast of forty days and forty nights the very mention of bread was a powerful temptation.

Satan knows all the appetites of our nature and tempts us accordingly. These appetites have their proper and natural uses; but it is Satan's sophistry to say, as so many are saying today, that it is never a sin to indulge an appetite, because God has implanted it in us. That was the trap into which our first parents fell. The forbidden fruit, the tempter told them, was good to eat. It would satisfy their hunger and would also make them wise as gods. That was the pit into which Esau fell when he despised his birthright and sold it for a mess of pottage to satisfy his hunger. "I am about to die," he said; "what good is my birthright to me?" That in substance is what every man who yields to the temptation of the flesh says, either before his trangression or after it. "God put this appetite in me and I will satisfy it." But that is not what the great souls said; not what Joseph said when he was tempted; not what Daniel or John the Baptist and other great souls said. They did not say, "A man must live, therefore I will do this wrong"; but rather, "The soul must live, even if the body should perish." And that was what Christ said here in the desert when He was tempted of the devil. "Man shall not live by bread alone, but by every word that proceedeth out of the mouth of the Lord."

Then there are the temptations to get profit or power, or attain some desire at the sacrifice of truth and right. This is powerfully illustrated in the Third Temptation of Jesus. This was the climax, the supreme effort of Satan. Here he threw off every pretense of seeming to persuade Christ to put his reliance upon God, and openly asked for His submission and worship. "He took Him to the top of an exceeding high mountain and showed Him all the kingdoms of the world and the glory of them, and said unto Him, All these things will I give Thee, if Thou wilt fall down and worship me."

Multitudes fall down before this temptation and are conquered by that dreadful and fatal "if" of Satan. "All this will I give thee, *IF* . . ." Not that they are offered all the kingdoms of this world as Satan offered them to Jesus, but that he offers them the particular thing they desire at the price of some dishonor or compromise with evil, which, in substance, is to fall down and worship Satan. There are thousands upon thousands who control and rule the appetites and passions of the flesh, but who, to get what they want, or to avoid and escape the difficult or the unpleasant, or to fulfill some urgent desire, will compromise with Evil and bow down to Satan.

Ever Satan is making that same proposition to the souls of men today that he made to Christ upon that exceeding high mountain; tempting them to be silent when they ought to speak; tempting them to lie or to leave out a part of the truth; tempting them to shut their eyes to sorrow and want; tempting them to make a profit or gain by deception or dishonesty. Multitudes, multitudes stand on their mountain of temptation and hear that seducive offer of Satan, "All this will I give thee—but upon this little condition—*if* thou wilt fall down and worship me." It was undoubtedly because of the power and prevalence of this temptation that Christ asked those memorable questions which had to do with the world and a man's soul, "What shall it profit a man, if he shall gain the whole world, and lose himself?"

II

OUR DEFENSE AGAINST TEMPTATION

We turn now from this discussion of the different kinds of temptation to a discussion of the means of defense against temptation.

One of the first and most important means of defense is a recognition of the reality of temptation, and of the great injury that temptation can do to our souls. No one can afford to be apathetic or indifferent who lives in a world of temptation. But with this recognition of the power and danger of temptation there should go also the acceptance of the truth that temptation can be resisted. You are not beaten before you go into battle. You are stronger than temptation if you want to be. I sometimes receive letters from tempted persons, who in their great distress write as if their fear were that when a particular temptation assails them they will go down before it. But this is not necessary for any soul. We have God's word on that matter, "There hath no temptation taken you save such as is common to man; for

God will not suffer you to be tempted above that you are able; but will with the temptation afford a way of escape, that ye may be able to bear it." When we realize this, when we say to ourselves, "It can be done"—"Temptation can be resisted and conquered," then we have put the soul on guard.

A second method of defense is to avoid exposing ourselves to temptation. Never hunt temptation; it will hunt you. Here the second temptation of Christ is a guide and a warning to us. The devil took Him up to a pinnacle of the Temple and, quoting the promise of one of the Psalms to Him, how angels would bear the believer up in their arms, told Him to cast Himself down from the Temple. But Christ answered, "Thou shalt not tempt the Lord thy God." There is such a thing as what we might call "tempting temptation." Christ prayed for His disciples that they might watch and pray for themselves lest they should *enter* into temptation. There is such a thing as *entering* into the dangerous territory of temptation. That territory is always dangerous, but especially so when we enter it ourselves. The Niagara River above the Falls is not a safe place for swimming. Much of the entertainment world today is an incitement to evil. It was not by accident that in Pompeii, as the ruins still show today, the houses of ill fame were built next to the theaters. The former depended upon the latter for their trade. Avoid, then, the places and persons and books and sights which Satan makes use of to tempt the soul.

One of the disciples of Plato, Trochilus, by almost a miracle had escaped from a storm at sea, in which the ship was sunk, and he himself almost perished. When he reached home, the first thing he did was to order his servants to wall up two windows in one of his chambers which looked out upon the sea. His fear was that on some fine, bright day, looking out upon the sea when it was calm and tranquil and flashing in the sunlight, he should again be tempted to venture upon its treacherous waters. There are not a few windows looking out upon the sea of temptation which the soul would do well to wall up.

Another important defence against temptation is to make immediate war upon temptation when it shows itself. The Germans have boasted about their Blitzkrieg, or lightning war, with which they demolished Poland, and with which they threaten to demolish England and France. Whatever we may think of that in international affairs, that is the only way to war on temptation. Make it a "Blitzkrieg," a lightning war. "Resist the devil, and he will flee from you." To debate with temptation, to parley with it, to hesitate for a single moment in the thought of the mind and the resolution of the heart, is to give temptation a great advantage in the battle which must follow.

Still another, and one of the most important means of defense, is to prepare in advance for the coming of temptation. One of the reasons why there is no panic or unmanning fright in Great Britain or in France today is that they long ago took into consideration the possibility of the present crisis and prepared themselves against attack. Their children have been evacuated from the great cities, their gas masks distributed, their bombproof shelters constructed, their valuable buildings sandbagged, their great centers blacked out at night, their anti-aircraft guns mounted. That careful and vigorous preparation has banished fear and fright, for they know they can give an account of themselves in the day of trial. In like manner, in this war that Satan brings against the soul by air, by land, by sea, and under the sea, by every instinct and appetite and desire and circumstance of human nature, a careful, godly, and prayerful living before temptation comes will prepare us for that war.

Men do not fall so suddenly as it seems. When a dam finally gives way, it looks as if it had gone out in a moment of time. But in reality that final giving away was only the last stage and incident in a long process of weakening and degeneration. So it is when the soul gives way. Beware, then, of what takes place in the hidden realm of thought and in the pool of imagination of thought and desire.

Christ said that Satan came and found nothing in Him. But with us when he comes he finds so often a door that has been left unlocked or a window open.

The Bible and prayer are important means of defense, not only when temptation strikes, but before it strikes. We say that Satan trembles when he sees the weakest saint upon his knees; but likewise he trembles when he sees the weakest saint open his Bible and read it. Remember that every day you go out into a world of moral peril. Prepare yourself for it by a few minutes with your Bible and a few moments on your knees.

Above all, live in the presence of Christ. Make him the Invisible Companion of your every day, and you will see how it is not mere poetry, what we sing in that old hymn, "Temptations lose their power, when Thou art nigh."

Temptation, which can do so much injury and hurt to a man, nevertheless, rested and conquered and overcome, can do great things *for* a man. In the Apocryphal Scriptures the angel said to Tobias, "Tobias, because thou wast acceptable to God, it was necessary that temptation should prove thee." An old-time preacher used to say that his blood ran cold when he would read that saying of the angel to Tobias; for if it was necessary for a good man like Tobias to be tempted to be acceptable to God, then what about a sinner like himself? But not only was it necessary for Tobias to be tempted, it was necessary for the Lord Jesus Christ Himself that He might become our Redeemer. It was His victory over temptation that fitted Him and qualified Him to be our Redeemer; and our victory, too, leads us on to higher things. In the Place Vendome you see the beautiful column of Napoleon's day fabricated out of the cannon taken in battle by the French armies. So the best and most useful things of life will be made out of the trophies taken in our battle with temptation.

"When the tempter came." That is the word with which the evangelists introduce the tremendous scene of Christ's temptation. But how beautiful and sublime is that word with which they conclude their account of the temptation,—"Behold, angels came and ministered unto Him." Sweet and pleasant will be the coming of those angels to the soul that resisted the tempter, and has said to him, "Get thee behind me, Satan." "Then the devil leaveth Him, and, behold, angels came and ministered unto Him."

IV

GETTING THE BEST OF ANGER

"Doest thou well to be angry?"

Jonah 4:9

AMONG the prophets, apostles, and patriarchs, who appear on the ceiling of the Sistine Chapel at the Vatican, there is none to whom Michelangelo gives a nobler countenance than Jonah. He was, indeed, a great prophet, although, so far as his history goes, he made a poor beginning and a poor ending. First, he tried to flee Tarshish, and thus evade his commission to preach repentance and judgment at the proud capital of the world's empire, Nineveh; and at the end of his story, we see him pass from the stage of Old Testament history in a fit of petulant anger. "Yet forty days, and Nineveh shall be destroyed," was the text of Jonah's sermon, as he walked through the streets of the great metropolis. Jonah did not expect, and apparently did not hope, that the Ninevites would repent. But that is what they did. From the king of Nineveh on his throne to the peasant in his hut, the whole population covered themselves with sackcloth and sat in ashes and fasted. "And God saw their works, that they turned from their evil way: and God repented of the evil which He said He would do unto them; and He did it not." God's judgments are always contingent upon repentance. There was no change in God's purpose, and when Nineveh repented, the city was saved from destruction.

This unexpected turn of events displeased Jonah and made him so angry that he asked God to take away his life. He said that when he was first commanded to go to Nineveh, but fled to Tarshish, it was because he knew that God was gracious and merciful and slow to anger. Now he had proved it. The sparing of Nineveh made Jonah feel that his preaching had been discredited. Angry with himself, and with Nineveh, and with God, Jonah went out to a hill in the suburbs of the city and sat down to see what would happen to Nineveh.

To shelter him from the sun, God provided him with a miraculous gourd, and the angry Jonah was much pleased with this shelter from the fierce glare of the Mesopotamian sun. But the next day, smitten with a worm, the gourd perished as quickly as it had arisen. Then the hot east wind began to blow, and Jonah, like to faint, again asked God to take away his life. Instead of doing so, God said to Jonah, "Come now, let us reason together. Doest thou well to be angry?" An angry man cannot see the truth, and Jonah replied at once, "I do well to be angry, even unto death." Then Jehovah said to him, "You are angry because the gourd, which you neither made nor created, and which came up in a night and perished in a night, was smitten with a worm. And should not I have regard for Nineveh, that great city, wherein are more than sixscore thousand persons?"

Jonah is an example of how the character of a good and a great man can be marred by anger, and his usefulness impaired. His story suggests the folly, the danger, and the injury of anger. Unfortunately, when a man is angry and gives unrestrained expression to his anger, as John did, his fellow men are not as patient and long-suffering, and do not always return the soft answer which God returned to the angry and petulant Jonah. Anger is one of the most common sins, yet one of the most dangerous and injurious to the peace and well-being of man. More than any other sin, it blasts the flower of friendship, turns men out of Eden, destroys peace and concord in the home, incites to crime and violence, and turns love and affection into hatred. The Bible is a great book. It holds the mirror up to nature. It has a great deal to say by way of personal illustration and explanation about the havoc wrought in human life by the sin of anger.

The first angry man who appears in the pages of the Bible was the first murderer, Cain. Christ warned men against being angry with their brother men, and the reason is that anger opens the way for crime and violence. It was so in the case of Cain. When the two brothers brought their offering, and, for some reasons not told us, God had respect for the offering of Abel, but not for the offering of Cain, Cain was very angry and his countenance fell. Here you have the natural history of anger and how it works—first in the heart, then in the face, and then in the deed. Envy, according to the New Testament, made Cain angry, and the anger born of envy and jealousy is always the most dangerous of passions. God reasoned with Cain, and said to him, as He said to Jonah, "Why art thou angry?" But Cain, like so many angry men, would not listen to reason, and in this fury heard only the voice of his own passion. Then and there was committed the first murder, when the soil drank the blood of Abel. What a trail of misery and crime and violence anger has left across the face of the earth, ever since angry Cain struck that first fatal blow and death entered the world to curse it! What happened to Cain in this instance, how he went out from the presence of the Lord a fugitive and a vagabond on the face of the earth, is a piece of history that angry men who have yielded to their passions have repeated over and over again. Anger drives men out and separates them from their fellow men. The angry man is the loneliest man.

The folly of anger is illustrated in the prophet Balaam, one of the most gifted and eloquent men of the Old Testament. When the eager Balaam, after apparently getting God's consent that he should go with the ambassadors of Balak, who wanted Balaam to come and curse the invading Israelites, was riding his ass along the highway toward Moab, and the angel of the Lord stood in the path with a drawn sword in his hand, he did not see the angel, and, enraged that the ass he was riding turned out of the path, fell to beating her with his staff. This only made matters worse, and the ass thrust herself against the wall and crushed the prophet's foot, whereupon Balaam renewed his blows and wished that he had a sword in his hand so that he might kill the ass. What a picture that is of a man losing his temper when confronted by adverse circumstances and venting his rage on even the brute creation, or even inanimate objects. Even an ass is wiser than a man under those circumstances; and we can well believe that the ass expostulated with the foolish Balaam. The real trouble was not with the ass, but with Balaam himself, for the angel of the Lord was there to rebuke him and to judge him. That is often the case; the man who is most violent in his anger at someone else really ought to be angry with himself, for he is the source of his own trouble and sorrow.

Another great man injured by anger was Moses. When the people murmured and asked for water,

Moses was commanded to strike the rock at Horeb. Out of all patience with the people and their waywardness, Moses struck the rock twice, as if the rock had been the head of the people, crying out as he did so, "Hear, ye rebels!" This burst of rage cost Moses the Promised Land, because it was for this transgression that Moses, in spite of his grand service and his pathetic pleading at the end of all Israel's wandering, was not permitted to go into the land of Canaan. That was not the first nor the last time that a land of promise and of happiness was lost through anger. Moses was not as patient as God. There is a legend that Abraham, sitting one day at the door of his tent at Mamre, was visited by a stranger, whom he invited to break bread with him. Unlike Abraham, the stranger did not pause before eating to ask God's blessing. Abraham inquired the reason why, and the stranger told him that he worshiped the sun. Very angry at this, Abraham drove the man out of his tent. Afterwards, the Lord called and asked where the stranger was. Abraham replied, "I thrust him out because he did not worship Thee." Then the Lord answered, "I have suffered him and his ancestors for hundreds of years, and couldst not thou endure him for one hour?"

Naaman, the great general and prime minister of Ben-Hadad, the King of Syria, is another instance of the folly of anger and the wisdom of putting anger aside in response to the invitation of friendship and judgment. He had come to Samaria from far-off Damascus with his chariots and a retinue of servants and costly presents to visit the great prophet Elisha, hoping that Elisha would cure him of his leprosy. To his astonishment and chagrin, Elisha would not even see him, but sent a servant out with a message to Naaman to go and wash himself seven times in the Jordan. This was humiliating for the great satrap of Syria. "Surely," he said, "I thought he would come out and pass his hand over the place and name the name of his God. Wash in the Jordan! If that's all that's necessary, there are plenty of rivers in Syria where I can wash. Are not Abana and Pharpar, rivers of Damascus, better than all the waters of Israel?" And with that, he brought his whip down on the flanks of his Arab steeds, and the chariot plunged forward on the road back to Damascus, leaving behind it a cloud of dust and the echo of Syrian imprecations. Fortunately for Naaman, he had sensible servants who talked with him and said, "My father, if the prophet had bid thee do some great thing, wouldst thou not have done it? how much rather then, when he saith to thee, Wash, and be clean?" Counseled by his servants, Naaman drove to the Jordan, dipped himself seven times as Elisha had directed, and his flesh came again unto him like the flesh of a little child, and he was clean. But how narrowly Naaman missed the great blessing through the indulgence of his anger because his pride had been wounded.

One of the unforgettable characters of our Lord is an angry man, the elder brother in the great tale of the two sons. When the prodigal had come home from the far country, and his rags had been burned in the stable yard, and the best robe put on him and a ring on his hand and shoes on his feet, and the fatted calf killed, and everyone had sat down at the table and the musicians had struck up a lively tune, the elder brother, coming in from the field, caught the sound of the music and dancing, and learning from one of the servants what it meant, he was angry and would not go in. His place was empty. At the table where his ought to have been the second seat of honor, he shut himself out from the banquet of reconciliation and forgiveness, and on what ought to have been, and could have been, the happiest day of his life, he was wretched and miserable and lonely, because he was angry and would not go in.

In a burst of anger one can destroy and undo what one has been laboriously building through many years. One of the old saints, greatly provoked, and explaining why he had not dealt more severely with wrongdoers who had been brought before him, said: "To tell you the truth, I feared to lose in a quarter of an hour the little gentleness that I have been laboring for twenty-two years to gather, drop by drop, like a shower in the vase of my poor heart." Friendships that are of long standing and whose branches have borne pleasant fruits can be blasted and withered by one unrestrained explosion of anger, for wounds can be inflicted and insults delivered, which, in a moment, the angry man would give all he possessed to recall; but the injury has been done and anger has provoked anger.

One of the saddest stories of the injury wrought by anger, and the remorse of an angry man, is the story of how Alexander the Great slew his friend and general, Clitus. Passing this summer over the highlands of Asia Minor, and visiting Ephesus and the Cilician Gates and Tarsus and Antioch, I thought much of the great conqueror who had passed that way. He was one of the few men who really deserved the adjective "great." His biographer describes him as by nature fervently passionate and impulsive. He was strong in his loves and in his loyalties; and although hatred was foreign to his magnanimous nature, he was often swept by storms of anger. Yet by a magnificent display of will power, he held the reins upon his passions. In the midst of the sensuous temptations of the Asiatic courts and the harem of Darius, he seems to have held himself in complete mastery and kept himself unspotted from the world.

But to this long chapter of noble self-control there

is one sad and tragic exception. At a banquet given for Dionysius, a song was sung comparing Alexander with Castor and Pollux, and to his advantage. Then someone disparaged the old Macedonian officers who had fought under Alexander's father, Philip. This roused one of Alexander's generals, Clitus, who commanded the famous Hetaeriae. Clitus reminded Alexander how he had saved his life in one of the recent battles, and told him he had bought his fame with the blood of the Macedonian officers. He told Alexander to associate with his lick-spittle Persians, who bowed the knee to him and told him only what he wanted to hear. Alexander, stung by this remark of Clitus, reached for his sword, which a discreet officer had hidden away. Then in his anger, falling, as men always do at such a time, into his native idiom, Macedonian, he ordered the trumpeter to sound the call, and when he delayed, smote him with his fist. Before he could inflict hurt upon Clitus, the friends of that half-intoxicated officer hurried him out of the banqueting hall. But he soon entered by another door, where he stood under the curtains, quoting lines from a Greek poet to the disparagement of Alexander's conquests. "Quick as a flash, Alexander snatched a spear from the hands of the guard and hurled it at the figure by a raised curtain. The deed was done. The friend of his childhood, his life companion and rescuer, lay gasping out his life." The passion of remorse followed quickly upon the fury of his anger. Alexander himself drew out the fatal spear, and but for his officers, would have fallen upon it. All through the night, and for several days, he lay writhing in his remorse, piteously calling Clitus by name and chiding himself as the murderer of his friend. Alexander the Great conquered the world, but he could not conquer himself. In his conquests he stormed and took almost every great city of the ancient world. Yet he was not able to subdue that city, to conquer which is the greatest of all achievements, the city and citadel of his own spirit.

When a man becomes angry, a wise friend can do him a great service. The attitude that we ought to take is that of God Himself, who reasoned with Cain, went out to talk with the angry elder brother, and said to Jonah, "Doest thou well to be angry?" See what benefit the servants of Naaman conferred upon him when they reasoned with him and persuaded him to put his rage aside. See what benefit the beautiful Abigail conferred upon David when she went to David, riding upon her ass, and in beautiful supplication and intercession dissuaded him from venting his murderous fury upon the churlish and ungrateful Nabal and all the people of his city.

"Grievous words stir up strife: but a soft answer turneth away wrath." It is said that when an elephant is enraged nothing calms him so well as a little lamb; and it is a well-known fact that Andrew Jackson in the battle of New Orleans stopped the cannon balls of the British artillery with bales of cotton.

Sometimes, as years increase and the difficulties of life increase, the occasions for anger are more frequent. Therefore the greater need that we should earnestly endeavor to conquer anger. The things which provoke, annoy, and irritate are, after all, God's ministers; they are elements and factors in our probation. Balaam beat his ass because she turned aside and crushed his foot against the wall; but he need not have been angry, for it was that which saved him from the avenging sword of the angel. Let us not be angry with adverse circumstances, because, somewhere in the midst of them, although hidden to our view, is the messenger and angel of God.

Above all, beware that the anger of the moment is not retained, and does not solidify into hatred. That is the saddest thing that can befall a human spirit. So the apostle said, "Be angry, and sin not: let not the sun go down upon your wrath." Do not give place to this devil of anger. But "resist the devil, and he will flee from you." Let your counselor, your friend, and your example be that One who, when He was reviled, reviled not again; and when He suffered, He threatened not.

V

GETTING THE BEST OF THE TONGUE

"Whoso keepeth his mouth and his tongue, keepeth his soul from troubles"

Proverbs 21:23

ALL races and literatures have proverbs on the power of the tongue. The Greek: "The boneless tongue, small and weak, can crush and kill." The Turk: "The tongue destroys a greater horde than does the sword." The Persian: "A lengthy tongue and early death." The Chinese: "The tongue can speak a word whose speed outstrips the steed." The Arab: "The tongue's great storehouse is the heart." But the Hebrew, the Bible, crowns them all: "Who keeps his tongue doth keep his soul."

It is not easy to keep the tongue, for "the tongue is an unruly member, full of deadly poison." Polonius asked Hamelt what he was reading. His reply was, "Words, words, words." Only words! And yet how great is the power of words! "Life and death are in the power of the tongue." It is impossible to calculate the injury wrought by an ungoverned and unconverted tongue. The iniquity of the tongue is a proof of the fall of man. The Apostle asks, "Doth a fountain send forth at the same place sweet water and bitter?" No fountain can do that, except one, and that is the fountain of the tongue, with which men bless God, and curse men who are made after the similitude of God.

"Words, words, words." Mere words! Words are as common as blossoms on a spring day; yet how mysterious their spell, how mighty their power, and how irrevocable their influence. Words are the transcript of the mind. A man's words are the index of this character. "Thy speech bewrayeth thee!" Homer used to speak of "winged" words, and his own words still wing their way in the firmament of human thought long centuries after they first commenced their flight. Of Martin Luther it was said that his words were battles. The prophets of God were commanded to take with them words, and their words still reverberate in the conscience of mankind. The words of Shakespeare were freighted with meaning. Whipple has declared that the finest prose sentence written on this side of the ocean is the following from Emerson's "Essay on Shakespeare": "One golden word leaps out immortal, from all this painted pedantry, and sweetly torments us with invitations to its own inaccessible home."

But most wonderful of all, most mysterious, most inexhaustible in their meaning, most inspiring, arresting, and comforting are the words of the Scriptures, the words of Jesus.

The Bible says that a word in season is good, that a wholesome tongue is a tree of life, and that life and death are in the power of the tongue. This power of words is confirmed by human experience. We have heard words spoken by a master of assemblies which thrilled us to the center of our being. We can recall words spoken to us in season which made the heart glad, and healed our wounds like oil; or words of counsel and warning; or words of exhortation and advice, which stirred our ambitions and started us on the right and profitable course. But we have heard words, too, which made us uncomfortable and unhappy, that discouraged us and depressed us; words that rankled and rasped and festered; words that opened doors to temptation; words that provoked us to wrath; words which, as St. James so powerfully said, set on fire the whole course of nature because they are set on fire of Hell.

Our Lord not only pronounced a judgment upon words, but He gives the reason for our accountability as to the words which we speak. The reason is that words tell the secret of the heart. A French cynic and diplomat said that words were intended to conceal thought. However that may be in diplomacy, it is not true in life. Words reveal thought and uncover the heart. "Out of the abundance of the heart the mouth speaketh. The good man out of his good treasure bringeth forth good things, and the evil man out of his evil treasure bringeth forth evil things." "Therefore," Christ says, "every idle word that men shall speak, they shall give account thereof in the day of judgment."

> "The deeds we do, the words we say,
> Into still air, they seem to fleet.
> We count them ever past,
> But they shall last,
> In the great Judgment Day,
> And we shall meet."

The words which we have whispered ever so softly will come back to us in the thunders of judgment and condemnation. Since all of us do more or less talking, it will not be without profit to think about our words and our responsibility for their use, and especially those words which bring us into judgment.

What does the wise man mean when he says that death is in the power of the tongue? He means that the tongue has the dread power to kill. How true that is. The tongue can kill happiness and friendship and hope and innocence and faith.

There are words of anger or enmity which stir up strife and sow the seeds of bitterness and hatred. A wound inflicted by the hand or by the sword will soon heal; but there are wounds inflicted by the tongue which never heal. These are the words that provoke one another to wrath and stir up the evil which sleeps in human nature. How many friendships have been broken, and homes saddened, and churches disrupted, and husbands and wives divorced, and nations set against nations by the power of evil words. The Apostle James did not overstate it when he said that the tongue is an unruly evil, "full of deadly poison," that "it defileth the whole body, and setteth on fire the course of nature, and is set on fire of hell."

Then there are words that stain and defile and corrupt the heart. Words can lead you heavenward, but they can also lead you into the infernal regions. Addison has a passage in *The Spectator* about the Roman Catholic doctrine of purgatory, how men must stay there until the influence of their evil writings has disappeared. But who can tell when that influence will come to an end? Only those who have occasion to deal with it in the courts know how immense and far-spread in this country is the business of sending out obscene literature. The motive is that of profit, but it is born out of an evil heart. It must be said, too, that there are widely circulated magazines and popular books which, while they escape conviction in the courts on the ground of obscenity, defile men's hearts and stain their imagination. It is a strange, but a true and a sad thing that the mind can easily forget a wholesome and beautiful and clean and helpful utterance, whereas some obscene tale or profane jest will lie year after year as a smudge on the mirror of the mind and will remain on the tablets of memory like the obscene pictures on the walls of Pompeii.

Among the words that have the power of death there are none so evil as the words of slander and defamation of character. When it comes to this kind of speech, the most vulgar, illiterate, and ill-disposed, who would not get a hearing on any other subject is sure to get a hearing when he speaks evil of others.

Slander shows its hideous speech, first of all, in the defamation of men in public life. In his life of Julius Caesar, James Froude writes: "The disposition to speak evil of men who have risen a few degrees above their contemporaries is a feature of human nature as common as it is base; and when to envy there is added fear or hatred, malicious anecdotes spring like mushrooms in a forcing pit."

> "He who ascends the mountain heights will find
>   The loftiest peaks most clothed in snow.
> And he who surpasses or subdues mankind
>   Must look down on the hate of men below."

After the battle of Antietam, Lincoln went down to visit McClellan and the army, remaining for four days and then returning to Washington. Soon an ugly undercurrent of rumor was flowing to the effect that Lincoln, driving over the battlefield, had asked for a comic and indecent song to be sung. In the political campaign of 1864 this was openly asserted. One of the chief papers of New York asserted that a day or two after the battle Lincoln was driving over the field with General McClellan, Colonel Lamon, his bodyguard, and some other officers. When they came to the stone bridge, Burnside's Bridge, where the dead lay in heaps, Lincoln, slapping the thigh of Lamon, exclaimed, "Lamon, give us that song about the 'Picayune Butler.' General McClellan has never heard it." Whereupon, McClellan raised his hand in deprecation, and said, "No, Mr. President, not now; anything but that here." With this for a start, one of the campaign songs for 1864 ran as follows:

> "Abe may crack his jolly jokes
>   O'er bloody fields of stricken battle,
> While yet the ebbing life tide smokes,
>   From men that die like butchered cattle.
> He, ere yet the guns grow cold,
> To pimps and pets may crack his stories."

Lincoln was greatly pained and distressed at the slander, and took the trouble to write a long account of what actually happened on the visit. This was to go as a letter from Lamon to one who had inquired as to the truth of the slander. However, Lincoln determined at the last to make no reply. But the letter tells what actually took place. On the visit to Antietam, the President, riding in an ambulance with McClellan and other officers, not a day or two after the battle, but two weeks after the battle, and where there was not a grave that had not been rained on since it was dug, in one of his melancholy moods asked Lamon to sing a little ballad called "Twenty Years Ago," and the singing of which Lamon said had often brought tears to Lincoln's eyes as he had listened to it on the circuit in Illinois or at the White House. The song commences,

> "I've wandered through the village, Tom,
> I've sat beneath the tree."

The ballad then goes on to relate the feelings of a man who returns to his native village after an absence of twenty years and finds everything changed and all his friends gone. This was the song for which Lincoln had asked. But at the conclusion of it, in order to lift him out of his melancholy, Lamon, at his own initiative, did sing the comic, but altogether harmless, song, "The Picayune Butler." These were the facts. Yet thousands believed that Abraham Lincoln was the sort of man who would call for a comic and indecent song when driving past the bodies of the men who had fallen in battle for the maintenance of the Union.

There is a school of biography abroad today which

can be briefly described as slanderous. Under the pretext that the history and biography must tell all that there is to be known about a man, whether good or evil, unsavory incidents in the lives of notable men are written and printed and circulated. An example of this is the recently published "Hidden Lincoln." No honorable purpose is served by the publication of incidents and facts which, even if true, stain the name of a great man and, if widely circulated, would hurt his abiding influence.

But worst of all is the slander of individuals in private life. This is sometimes done out of pure malice or envy. We may be reluctant to think that it is so, but there are men like those described in the Apocalypse, "who make and love a lie." They create the lie and they love to circulate it. "The poison of asps," as the Psalmist said, "is under their tongue." If you ever have occasion to doubt the fall of man and the ruin of his nature by sin, remember this fact about human nature.

A man can be slandered not only by the telling of what is false, but by the distortion and misrepresentation of what is true, or by telling of something less than the whole truth. That was the way the wretched Doeg slandered the innocent high priest, Ahimelech, when he told the enraged Saul that the priest had fed and armed David, but omitted to say that Ahimelech thought that David was on an errand for the king.

The original liar and slanderer could do little damage and make little headway in his evil campaign, were it not for the assistance which he receives from careless and thoughtless persons, who, with no particular malice in their heart, and no definite purpose of injury to others, yet delight to hear and to pass on an evil report. So the tale passes from mouth to mouth, until an endless chain of calumny has been fabricated. Did you ever upset a bottle of ink on a white cloth, or on a white blotter, and see its slow but inexorable spread? So the evil tale, once told, spreads further and further, until a good name is blackened.

A great preacher, Bishop Simpson, speaking on this theme, and especially the slander of Christian men, once said, "I would rather play with the forked lightning, or take in my hands living wires with their fiery currents, than speak a reckless word against any servant of Christ, or idly repeat the slanderous darts which thousands of Christians are hurling on others to the hurt of their own souls and bodies." Then he goes on to say that the reason why Christians sometimes are not filled with joy, are not blessed and prosperous in their life, may be that "some dart which you have flung with angry voice, or in an idle hour of thoughtless gossip, is pursuing you on its way

as it describes a circle which always brings back to
the source from which it came every shaft of bitterness and every evil and idle word."

Slander is an injury which it is hard to undo, even
when one might desire to do so. A peasant had slandered a friend, only to find out that what he had
said was not true. Troubled in his conscience, he
went to a monk to seek advice. The monk said to
him, "If you want to make peace with your conscience, you must fill a bag with feathers and go to
every dooryard in the village and drop in each of
them one feather." The peasant did as he was told,
and returning to the monk announced that he had
done penance for his sin. "Not yet!" said the monk
sternly. "Take up your bag, go the rounds again,
and gather up every feather that you have dropped."
"But," exclaimed the peasant, "the wind has blown
them all away by this time!" "Yes, my son," answered the monk, "and so it is with gossip and slander. Words are easily dropped, but no matter how
hard you try, you never can get them back again."

If the Old Testament portrait of the noble man is
that of a man who will not take up an evil reproach
against his neighbor, certainly it is the portrait of
the noble New Testament man, where love, we are
told, covers a multitude of sins. An "evil reproach"
should be spoken only when it is true, and then only

when the speaking of it is necessary for the safe-
guarding of honor and virtue. Never otherwise!

Fathers and mothers here tonight may sometimes
think that even your best efforts and example have
little effect upon your children. But be not deceived
or discouraged. Something that you have done or
said will ever be before your child when you have long
been in your grave. One thing that I remember about
my own father is that I never heard from his lips a
word of evil report or detraction concerning any man,
either in public or in private life, save once; and that
one exception was when the truth had to be spoken
in order to warn and to safeguard his children. The
cure for defamation, gossip, and slander is a con-
verted soul, and the love of Christ in the heart.
Then, instead of delighting in dragging out, exposing, and exaggerating the faults of others, we shall
do what we can to cover them with the mantle of
charity.

> "Teach me to feel another's woe,
> To hide the fault I see;
> That mercy I to others show,
> That mercy show to me."

On the great Hall of Man at the New York's
World's Fair one saw inscribed the words of St.
Augustine, "Man wanders o'er the earth, and wonders at the restless sea, the flowing waters, the sight
of sky; but forgets that of all wonders man himself

is the most wonderful." Yes! Man is fearfully and wonderfully made, and the most wonderful thing about man is his power of speech, the power to express in words the basest or the noblest desires of his nature and the thoughts of his mind. If, as the wise man said, the power of death is in the tongue, likewise also is the power of life. Live in the fellowship of Christ, and your tongue will speak the words of purity and truth, of encouragement, of hope, of faith, words that endure forever and which will echo sweetly for you in the day of judgment. Speak those words, and speak them Now, while it is called Today. Do not wait until death palsies the tongue. Sometimes when I stand, as I often must, by the side of the dead, and look down upon the still face and the now forever closed lips of the dead, that is what I wonder—If those lips could open again, if the tongue could speak once more, what would it say? What spoken word would it recall? What unspoken word would it make haste to utter? "Lord, speak to me, that I may speak in living echoes of Thy tone."

VI

GETTING THE BEST OF TROUBLE

"It is good for me that I have been afflicted"
Psalm 119:71

"Thou hast enlarged me when I was in distress"

Psalm 4:1

To get the best of trouble is one of life's most important victories, for trouble is sure to come. Trouble is as universal as human nature. "Man is born to trouble as the sparks fly upward." Trouble is no respecter of persons; it knocks at the door of millionaire and peasant, philosopher and illiterate, believer and unbeliever. Job's famous metaphor, that man is born to trouble as the sparks fly upward, is a true description of this side of our life. Light a brush fire at the eventide and then watch the sparks as they fly upward! They are the inevitable result and accompaniment of the fire. Likewise, wherever the fire of life is lighted, wherever a man passes through the experiences of this world, upward fly the sparks of trouble.

There are all kinds of trouble. Troubles of the body, troubles of the mind, troubles of the soul; the troubles we bring upon ourselves, and the troubles others bring upon us; sorrow, loneliness, fear, remorse, pain, sin. No man is exempted, and in this warfare which is appointed unto man there is no discharge. Sometimes those who seem to have the fewest troubles will have the most. Like the King of Samaria who wore his sackcloth of distress within, many who present to the world a fair, unruffled surface have deep trouble within. An unknown author has said:

"If every man's internal care
Were written on his brow,
How many who our envy share
Would have our pity now."

Always the army of the troubled is passing by. Early in the morning the streets and sidewalks of the city begin to resound with the marching feet of the toilers and the buyers and sellers. At noon the chorus reaches its loudest volume. Then the sound begins to decrease, until midnight comes, when, save for the nightwatchman and the night reveler, the streets are deserted. But the sound of the marching feet of the army of the troubled never ceases. Morning, noon, evening, and midnight, I hear them marching by in an endless procession. March! March! March!

The barometer lets you know when the storm is coming. The warning siren lets you know when the air-raider is coming; but trouble comes without a trumpet, unheralded and unexpected. Nothing, therefore, can be more important than to get the best of trouble, which gets the best of so many souls in life.

I

TROUBLE IS A DIVINE APPOINTMENT

One way to get the best of trouble is to realize that it is permitted by God, and, in that sense, is appointed by Him. There are no chances and no accidents in God's providential rule of my life. He makes no mistakes. In His Eternal Plan there are no errors. He selects the particular trouble which is best suited for us. When in any trouble, it is well to remember that of thousands of different kinds of trouble, this is the one which God has selected for you. I remember a devout friend saying of another friend, who was passing through a very keen distress, that she always believed God sent trouble for a purpose, but that in this particular case she wondered why this trouble was appointed for this friend. But it is not necessary for us to know why. That old saint of Scotland, Samuel Rutherford, once in deep distress was tempted to murmur and almost gave up hope. But ere long he was given comfort and strength in his distress, and began to see the purpose of it. It was then he wrote that we must never try to read God's messages through the envelope in which they come. He meant that it takes time for God's purpose to be made clear to us. "Fool that I was," wrote Rutherford, "not to know that the messages of God are not to be read through the envelope in which they are enclosed." Sometimes,

"Not till the loom is silent
And the shuttles cease to fly,
Shall God unroll the canvas
And explain the reason why
The dark threads are as needful
In the weaver's skillful hand
As the threads of gold and silver
In the pattern He has planned." [1]

The great mathematician, theologian, and saint, Blaise Pascal, in a letter written to a friend who was passing through deep waters, instead of using the stock phrases of consolation, advised him to seek his comfort in the eternal decree of God. "If we follow this precept, and if we regard this event not as an effect of chance, not as a fatal necessity of nature, but as a result indispensable, inevitable, just and holy, of a decree of His Providence, conceived from all eternity, to be executed at such an hour and in such a manner, we shall adore in humble silence the impenetrable loftiness of His Secrets; we shall venerate the sanctities of His Decrees, we shall bless the acts of His Providence, and uniting our will to that of God Himself, we shall wish with Him and for Him the thing that He has willed in us and for us from all eternity."

[1] Author unknown.

II

IN TROUBLE CALL UPON GOD

Since trouble does not come without God's permission and appointment, we can call upon God to give us strength and hope in the midst of trouble. The Psalmist said, "It is good for me to draw near unto God. I have put my trust in the Lord, that I may declare all Thy works."

When Robinson Crusoe was taken sick on his lonely isle, and was faint in body and fainter still in spirit, rummaging one day through an old chest which he had salvaged from the wreck, and searching for a medicine, he came upon a Bible. After he had taken the medicine, he opened the Bible, and the first verse upon which his eye fell was this from the 50th Psalm, "Call upon Me in the day of trouble: I will deliver thee; and thou shalt glorify Me." This produced a great impression upon Robinson, and he began to hope that perhaps God would heal him of his sickness, and deliver him from his solitary island and bring him back to his native land and to his friends once more. Before he went to bed that night, he did what he had never done before, knelt down and prayed, and in his prayer asked God that he would fulfill the promise of that verse in his own life and heal him of his sickness and deliver him from his wave-washed island. After that he sank into an untroubled sleep. Some days afterwards, as he was walking along the shore with his gun over his shoulder, his heart almost came to a stop, when he saw on the sand the imprint of a foot of a savage. He fled to his stockade and, climbing over the wall, pulled the ladder in after him in the greatest fear and terror. Then those same words came to him again, "Call upon Me in the day of trouble: I will deliver thee," and as he remembered them his fear began to leave him.

We are all mariners on the sea of life, and sometimes cast upon islands of distress. When that happens, the thing to do is what Robinson Crusoe did, call upon God in the day of trouble. That was what Hezekiah did when he got the blasphemous letter from Sennacherib's lieutenant, threatening destruction to Jerusalem and to all the people of God. He took the letter into the temple, the place of prayer, and "spread it out before the Lord." And God heard him and delivered him and delivered Israel. That is what David did in his time of trouble. "In my distress I called upon God, and He heard me." That is what Paul did when the ship was driving through the Mediterranean, and God sent His angel to the rescue. Prayer is to the soul in time of trouble what a life jacket is to the shipwrecked passenger.

> "From every stormy wind that blows,
> From every swelling tide of woes,

There is a calm, a sure retreat:
'Tis found beneath the Mercy Seat."

"Ah! whither could we flee for aid,
When tempted, desolate, dismayed;
Or how the hosts of hell defeat,
Had suffering saints no Mercy Seat?"

III

THE GOOD THAT COMES OUT OF TROUBLE

Since trouble comes by divine appointment, we can have faith that there is good to be derived from it. First of all, good for ourselves. "It is for my good that I have been afflicted," said the Psalmist, who more than any other in the Bible touches the chords of the human heart. And in another place he says, "Thou hast enlarged me when I was in distress."

There is, indeed, an enlarging power in trouble. It can give us strength, which hitherto we did not possess, to break the bonds of some sinful habit. It can reveal to us our selfishness, our lack of faith and piety, and so bring us nearer to God. That is what the hymn writer must have meant, when in her famous hymn she wrote,

"Out of my stony griefs
Bethel I'll raise;
So by my woes to be
Nearer, my God to Thee,
Nearer to Thee."

Horace Bushnell, one of the great preachers and

theologians of the last century, said that the death of his child had taught him more experimental theology than all his years of study. As the sandal tree scents with its pleasant savor the axe that fells it, so we have a right to expect that trouble will bless and enlarge our life. As Jacob struggling with the angel cried, "I will not let thee go except thou bless me," let us determine that trouble shall not pass over us without a blessing to our life.

In trouble there is to be found good for others also—that is, through us, for others. That is a question that we ought to ask when trouble has come, or when its tempest has passed by—What new power, what new influence has it bestowed upon me?

Trouble ought to increase our sympathy. It was when Harriet Beecher Stowe sat through the long nights in her home on the campus of Lane Theological Seminary at Walnut Hills, Cincinnati, watching the struggles of a dying child, that she began to think about the sorrows of slave mothers who were parted from their children by the cruel practice of the age. And then it was that there was born within her the desire to write the great book, *Uncle Tom's Cabin*, that did so much to bring the wrongs and the sorrows of the slave to the attention of the world.

In Jerusalem today there is an institution known as the American Colony, founded to help little children in the city where our Saviour died. And this is how it came to be. A well-to-do, beautiful, and talented young woman, resident in Chicago, was crossing the Atlantic on her way to visit her aged parents in Paris. On the journey the steamer was struck amidships by a large sailing vessel, and immediately began to sink. The four daughters who were with this woman were drowned, but she herself was rescued. When she reached land she sent a cable back to her husband in Chicago, "Saved alone!" Then she began to think about that word "alone," and accepting her great sorrow in the death of her children, and her own deliverance from death, as a divine message, she resolved to give her life to the welfare of her fellow passengers on life's long voyage, and so established the Colony in Jerusalem, which has brought the knowledge and the Spirit of Christ to so many of the children and youth of the Holy Land.

In the bitter political campaign of 1884, James G. Blaine was attacked as a corruptionist and Grover Cleveland as an immoral man. In the midst of the campaign the great American preacher, Henry Ward Beecher, took the stump in behalf of Cleveland. The reason was that, having suffered himself so deeply through slander, Beecher had resolved to defend, if he could, any man who was assailed in a like manner. At a great meeting at the Brooklyn Rink on October 22, Beecher said: "When in the gloomy night of my own suffering I sounded every depth of sorrow, I vowed that if God would bring the Daystar of Hope, I would never suffer brother, friend, or neighbor to go unfriended should a like serpent seek to crush him. This oath I will regard now because I know the bitterness of venomous lies. I will stand against infamous lies that seek to sting to death an upright man and magistrate." Thus Beecher found honey for the good of others in the carcass of slander.

When John Bright spoke at the dedication at the Cobden Memorial at Leamington in England, he revealed a hitherto unknown chapter in the relationship between himself and that other great reformer, Richard Cobden. In the speech he said: "I was in despair, for the life and sunshine of my house had been extinguished. All that was left on earth of my young wife, except the memory of a sainted life and a too brief happiness, was lying still and cold in the chamber above us. Mr. Cobden called upon me as a friend and addressed me as you may suppose in words of condolence. After a time, he looked up and said: 'There are thousands of houses in England at this moment where wives, mothers, and children are dying of hunger. Now when the first paroxysm of your grief has passed, I would advise you to come with me and we will never rest until the Corn Law is repealed.' I accepted his invitation. Since then, though there has been suffering, and much suffering in many houses in England, yet no wife and no mother and no little

child has starved to death as the result of a famine
made by law."

In the deep waters of his own anguish and sorrow
John Bright sowed the harvest for the suffering poor
of England.   God enlarged him in the time of his
distress.   In after years he looked back to this period
when it had seemed to him that the very light of his
life had gone out, and confessed in faith and gratitude, "My God knew best."

On the shores of the Baltic Sea, after a great
storm, the fishermen go down into the water and rake
the beach for the precious ambergris which has been
cast upon the shores by the tumult of the waves.
Life's storms bring their treasures with them, and
we are wise fishermen if we go out after the waves and
billows have passed over us and gather up the heaven-
ly ambergris with which they have strewn the shores
of our life.

VII

GETTING THE BEST OF YESTERDAY

"Forgetting those things which are behind"

Philippians 3:13

PAUL himself is a magnificent illustration of a man who got the best of yesterday. There was much that was dark and sinful and sad in Paul's Yesterday, much that as a follower of Christ he would like to forget and turn away from forever. In that Yesterday were his persecutions of the Church of Christ, his blasphemies, his cruelties toward those who believed in Christ. But Paul nobly conquered, forgot, left behind, and got the best of all that was dark and bitter and sad in his past. It was he who left us out of his own great experience and out of his own autobiography this ever-resounding and deathless text, "Forgetting the things which are behind," and that other great text, too, forged out of his own experience, "All things work together for good to them that love God."

In certain respects we are all like the Apostle Paul. We all have much that ought to be forgotten. It may be a sorrow, a hurt, a wound, a bitter experience, or transgression and sin; but in Jesus Christ we have the great liberty to forget; we can do all things through

Him; and one of the greatest things we can do in Him is to forget the things that are behind. Yesterday, the past, is one of man's greatest enemies. One of the greatest blessings that Christian faith bestows upon us is this ability to forget the past.

I

GETTING THE BEST OF THE SORROWS, LOSSES, AND INJURIES OF THE PAST

Our first sermon in this series dealt with Fear, and how to get the best of this great enemy of peace and happiness. Fear has to do with Tomorrow; but in this sermon we deal with Yesterday. How many are the victims of Yesterday! Sometimes I am not sure whether Yesterday or Tomorrow is man's greatest foe.

There are a great many who are unable—or rather unwilling, for in Christ all are able—to get the best of the sorrows and bereavements of yesterday. They permit their mind to turn back to a sorrow or loss, until they are unfitted for the duties of life, unhappy and discontented themselves, and of no help to others. There is no objection to thinking of those who have departed. We all do that, and such thoughts will often comfort and guide and purify and inspire. But what is wrong and unfortunate, when we think of the departed, is that we should think only of the loss that we sustained when they were taken away from us, and forget the blessing that their life bestowed upon us. In that connection, the great and beautiful gratitude and resignation of afflicted Job come to mind, after he had lost all his property and all his children, too—"The Lord gave, and the Lord hath taken away; blessed be the Name of the Lord!" When you think of your friends who have been taken from you, do not be so selfish and ungrateful in the presence of God as to mourn only for their passing, but rejoice also in their life, their counsel, their affection, and their memory. When God has taken away a loved one, do not, in the pain of separation, forget that first of all God gave.

One of the noblest characters in the Old Testament is Samuel. In his whole life there is only once even the faintest suggestions of a fault, and perhaps even that fault "leaned to virtue's side." The only rebuke Samuel ever received from God was for his intemperate sorrow over the fall of Saul. Once we are told that he wept all night for Saul; and after his last meeting with that unfortunate king he mourned constantly for him; mourned for him because he had anointed him with his own hands, and because he knew his great parts and his better and nobler nature. Then God said to Samuel, "How long wilt thou mourn over Saul, seeing I have rejected him from being king over Israel?" There are two things in that rebuke that God spoke to Samuel which those who mourn intemperately should remember. In the first place,

Samuel's grief was useless. God had rejected Saul and had chosen another to take his place. In the second place, Samuel's continued mourning for Saul showed a lack of submission to the will and appointment of God, and also unfitted Samuel for the spiritual leadership of Israel.

The great sorrow of Abraham Lincoln's life was the death of his son Willie, who died at the White House on February 20, 1862. This sorrow almost crushed the President. For a time he observed every Thursday, the day on which the child died, as a day of mourning, and separated himself from public duties. It was necessary for his friends to go to him and persuade him to give up that useless and dangerous habit. Lincoln learned to subordinate his personal sorrow to his public duties, although always afterward he wore his "sackcloth within."

In the life of General Sherman we have the story of how he conquered a great sorrow for the sake of duty and of country. His boy Willie, who had come down with his mother to visit Sherman after victory at Vicksburg, was taken ill on a steamboat going up the Mississippi River and died in Memphis at the Gayoso Hotel on October 3, 1863. The boy was a great favorite with the soldiers and dearly beloved by his father, who sometimes took him to ride with him when he reviewed the troops. The night of his death Sherman wrote to an intimate friend, Capt. C. C.

Smith: "The child that bore my name, and in whose future I reposed with more confidence than I did my own plan of life, now floats a mere corpse, seeking a grave in a distant land, with a weeping mother, brother, and sisters clustered about him. For myself, I ask no sympathy. On, on, I must go to meet a soldier's fate, or live to see our country rise superior to all factions, till its flag is adored and respected by ourselves and by all the powers of the earth."

Perhaps the grandest instance of conquering sorrow for the sake of duty is found in the history of Ezekiel. The Word of the Lord came to him saying that his wife was to be taken from him with a stroke. Ezekiel refers to her with words which are full of heartbreak as the "desire of my eyes." Under this crushing sorrow he was to make no outward show of mourning. He was to sigh, but not aloud. His grief was not to interfere with his public duties as prophet. The symbolic significance of the grief of Ezekiel in connection with the fall of Jerusalem does not interest us, but the personal heroism of it does. "At even my wife died," he says, *and in the morning I did as God commanded.*" Always for all of us there is the morning of Duty. In the morning!

There are a great number, too, who are the victims of the painful and unpleasant experiences of the past. They are always turning back to some unhappy thing in their past. Someone hurt them, or wounded them, or deceived them, or injured them in some way, and they are never able to get over it, and that one event of the past is like a slave driver to their souls. They are victims in a double sense. There was first of all the hurt, or wound, or injury of the past, and, in the second place, the constant resurrection of it by their unrestrained grief over it and their ever turning back to it.

All of us have enough in our past in the way of sorrow, or hurt, or wounds, or injury, or disappointment, which, were we constantly to dwell upon it, would poison our spirit and disqualify us for the work of life. Far wiser was the plan of Joseph, the hero of the Bible's greatest story. No man had suffered greater hurt, or wound, or wrong, or sorrow than had Joseph. He was sold for a slave by his cruel and angry brothers into Egypt and there falsely charged with an infamous crime and unjustly imprisoned. But in a better day, when his two sons were born to him, he named one of them Manasseh, "for God hath made me forget all my toil"; and the name of the second son he called Ephraim, "for God has caused me to be fruitful in the land of my affliction." Joseph is more like a Christian than any man in the Old Testament; and in his ability to forget wrongs and injuries and to recognize that even in such things God had a blessing for his life, he shows a triumphant Christian spirit. Later on, when his brethren came to him and feared that he would take vengeance on them after the death of their father, Joseph forgave them and said, "As for you, ye meant evil against me; but God meant it unto good." That is the way to remember, and also forget, the hard and bitter things of the past, to see the hand of God in them and to trust that He meant it for good.

> "Who bears in mind misfortunes gone,
>   Will live in fear of more:
> The happy man whose heart is right
>   Gives no such shadows power.
>
> "He bears in mind no haunting past,
>   To vex his week on Monday.
> He has no graves within his mind
>   To visit every Sunday."

II

THE SINS AND TRANSGRESSIONS AND FAILURES OF THE PAST

How can we forget the sins and transgressions and moral failures of yesterday? Yet Paul said he had. He said that he forgot the things that were behind. And if he could, so can you and I. This does not mean that the way of the transgressor is not hard. Retribution is part of God's law for the universe; but in Christ all things are possible, and even past sin can be remembered only as an event that has led to a disclosure of God's love and goodness and as a means of purifying our souls. So the great poet and artist, William Blake, said, when he thought of his past transgression, "O Mercy, O Divine Humanity, O Forgiveness and Pity and Compassion! If I were pure, I should never have known thee. If I were not polluted, I should never have glorified thy holiness or rejoiced in thy great salvation." There is said to be a liquid which, poured upon dust and rubbish, can make it shine like precious stones. What in chemistry and metallurgy is only a fable, is not a fable when it comes to God's dealing with the heart of man. The forgiveness of God in Christ transfigures even the dust and ashes of our sins and makes them to glow with the light of heaven.

In a sermon last spring I told of a man who once came to me and said that he would like to help in the Church, but didn't dare to. Then he went on to relate the history of the sad and unfortunate incident of his life. Should he now come forward and make a public profession of his faith and engage in the work of the Church, he felt that accusation might be brought against him, and that the unfortunate incident and transgression of the past would be dragged into the light, to his own distress, to the distress of others, and to the injury of the Church.

Here was a man who was ruled and enslaved by the past. He feared that if he came out into the open and spoke for Christ, the dead hand of the past would be stretched out and placed with restraining and accusing power upon his shoulder. This man was representative of a class more numerous than we think. There is no doubt about the tyranny of the past and that a man's transgressions come back to fight against him. The question is, How can we deal with the past? Is it possible to throw off its tyranny and get strength and power out of our past instead of weakness? The great answer of Christianity is that we can. The forgiveness of God delivers us from the bondage of the past. That was the great experience of St. Paul. His sinful, persecuting, blaspheming past, instead of silencing him and paralyzing his energies, only served to make him a more powerful and persuading and eloquent ambassador of the forgiving and restoring grace of God.

That, too, was the experience of Peter. How shameful and despicable his profane disavowal and denial of Jesus, just at the time that He needed most the love and loyalty of His friends! And yet, when the love of Christ had restored Peter and forgiven him, and sent him out to feed the flock of God and to preach the gospel, Peter overcame his past. The memory of his dark transgression now only served to deepen and enlarge his conception of the love of God and gave him eloquence as he proclaimed it to the world. There is an old legend that sometimes when Peter was preaching he would hear the crowing of a cock nearby, and would halt and stumble in his sermon as he remembered that fearful night when he heard the cock crow after he had denied his Lord. But in a moment or two, recovering his composure, he would go on preaching with greater power and earnestness than ever.

In the book of Joel there occurs this great verse: "I will restore to you the years that the locust hath eaten." It was a word spoken to Israel at the time of a terrible invasion of locusts. Like an army with the rattle of war chariots, the locusts swarmed in on the land, devouring the orchards and vineyards and fields, and when they departed left the land wasted like a desert and the fountains and wells polluted. Joel called upon the people to repent that the judgment of God might be turned away. When the wind blew from another direction, the locusts were swept away, some to the Dead Sea and some to the Mediterranean, and the place that once knew them now knew them no more forever. But what of the blasted vineyards, the bare and bleeding trees, and the locust-eaten herbs? The promise is that the land shall be restored. The beasts of the field are assured that the pastures of the wilderness will spring again, and the fig tree and the vine yield their strength. The people are told to rejoice because God will bring down the former and the latter rain, and the floor shall be full of wheat again, and the vats shall overflow with wine and oil. "I will restore to you the years that the locust hath eaten."

A beautiful promise that! Human life is often eaten by sin, as the land of Israel was by the locusts. There are many names for sin, and many forms of sin; but sin is always the same in its blighting work upon the soul. Who is there that will not know some locust-eating year? If there was not definite transgression, there were unspiritual and unresponsive moods. There were times when we were led by the whisper of desire, or prompted by unkind and ungenerous feelings. Here and there, as we turn the pages of life's diary, across this or that page we shall be compelled to write "Locust years."

But the grace of God in the penitent and contrite soul is able to undo what sin has done and to restore the years that the locust hath eaten. What a message of hope and encouragement that is; that all the losses, the hurts, the shocks, the bleedings of heart, the scorchings and scars of sin, can be annulled and wiped out by the grace of God! This does not mean that the way of the transgressor is not hard. Even Calvary's agony cannot make it easy. But if the Bible teaches the terrible effects of sin, it also teaches that a man is not forever bound and crippled by sin. The Greek idea of retribution was that nobody, not even a god, could escape from himself or change his heart. But the Christian idea of forgiveness is that even the humblest sinner by repentance and by faith can escape the final penalty of sin, and have all the losses inflicted by sin restored.

The Bible abounds in instances of men whose locust years were restored and who were permitted to forget their past: the aged King Manasseh, who, after fifty years of unprecedented wickedness and impiety, came to himself and repented and was forgiven and restored again to his throne; and David, who, after his triple and terrible sin of adultery and murder and treachery, his heart broken by Nathan's beautiful parable of the little lamb, repented and was forgiven, and now forever teaches transgressors the ways of God; and Peter, too, who cursed his Lord, but when he had repented and was restored and forgiven, became the leader of the Church; and Paul, fierce blasphemer and persecutor, who, after Christ appeared to him at Damascus, preached the Christ he had once persecuted, and labored more abundantly than all the apostles, and looked now upon his past history and his miraculous conversion, and the wonderful mercy that God had shown, as God's plan that "in him first Jesus Christ might show forth all long-suffering, for a pattern to them which should hereafter believe on Him to life everlasting." That is, Paul made use of his own past experience to demonstrate to the world the power of Christ to save even to the uttermost.

The past is conquered when a man turns it over to Christ. Here are three verses which I once repeated on a Sunday night, and heard by a man and his wife were used for their conversion. Perhaps they will help someone here tonight. They deal with the story of a man who applied to a prominent manufacturer for a position. When he did so, he felt bound to tell him of an unfortunate chapter in his past. "Never mind," said the manufacturer; "I don't care about the past. Start where you stand."

"Start where you stand and never mind the past;
   The past won't help you in beginning new.
If you have left it all behind at last,
   Why, that's enough: you're done with it, you're through.
This is another chapter in the book,
   This is another race that you have planned.
Don't give the vanished days a backward look—
   Start where you stand.

The world won't care about your old defeats,
   If you can start anew and win success;
The future is your time, and time is fleet,
   And there is much of work and strain and stress;
Forget the buried woes and dead despairs;
   Here is a brand new trial right at hand;
The future is for him who does and dares—
   Start where you stand.

Old failures will not halt, old triumphs aid;
   Today's the thing, tomorrow soon will be;
Get in the fight and face it unafraid,
   And leave the past to ancient history;
What has been, has been; yesterday is dead,
   And by it you are neither blessed nor banned.

[95]

Take courage, man, be brave and drive ahead—
  Start where you stand!" [1]

Two brothers were once convicted of stealing sheep,
and in accordance with the brutal punishment of that
day were branded on the forehead with the letters
"S T," which stood for "sheep thief." One of the
brothers, unable to bear the stigma, wandered from
land to land, and at length, full of bitterness, died
and was buried in a forgotten grave.

But the other brother, who repented of his mis-
deed, did not go away from his home. He said to
himself, "I can't run away from the fact that I stole
sheep, and here I will remain until I win back the
respect of my neighbors and myself." As the years
passed by, he established a reputation for respecta-
bility and integrity. One day a stranger in the town
saw the old man with the letters "S T" branded on
his forehead, and asked a native what they signified.
After thinking for a little time, the villager said, "It
all happened a great while ago, and I have forgotten
the particulars; but I think the letters are an ab-
breviation of Saint."

Yes, that is it! The wonderful grace of God in the
penitent and believing heart is able to change and
transform the odious marking and scarring of sin
into a badge of honor and of beauty.

[1] Copyright by Berton Braley.

VIII

GETTING THE BEST OF LONLLINESS

"... Alone"

Isaiah 63:3

Now I am all alone."
I sat with the physician in his library speaking the
usual words of sympathy and condolence. He gave
me a brief history of his sister's illness, their past
fellowship, and then concluded with these words, "I
am all alone now." On the desk was the framed
photograph of a beautiful woman. I lifted it, and
glancing at it, said to him, "Another sister?" "No,"
he answered as the shadow of another earlier, perhaps deeper, sorrow came over his face. Then again
he said, "I am all alone now."

His words followed me to the vestibule, down the
steps, around the corner, down the avenue, and back
to my own home. Sometimes as I pass down the
crowded street and see some face shrouded with loneliness, and how many such there are in the great city
with its teeming thousands, or as I have spoken a
word of encouragement and sympathy to one who has
been left to be brave alone, those words of that physician spoken to me as he sat there, with his pale face
lighted up by the lamp of his library, have come back
to me, "Now I am all alone."

"Alone—that worn-out word,
  So idly spoken and so coldly heard;
  Yet all that poets sing and grief hath known
  Of hopes laid waste dwells in that word, 'Alone.'"

Any series of sermons on this subject, FACING LIFE AND GETTING THE BEST OF IT, without a sermon on loneliness, would be obviously incomplete, for loneliness is one of the deepest shadows cast upon our world. There is no doubt that a great part of the appeal, the universal appeal, of Robinson Crusoe, is not in his adventures and his clever devices to arrange and regulate his life, but in his loneliness. That strikes a universal chord. The King of Persia, Ahasuerus, once gave orders that no man wearing sackcloth should appear before his palace. He did not wish to be reminded of the fact that there were miserable and unhappy people in his realm. But a church ought to have this one advantage over all other places of public assembly, in that it is the place where we face the facts of life, all of them, and consider those facts in the light of the Divine Revelation.

Perhaps one of the best ways to get at this subject will be to speak of the different kinds of loneliness which the human soul experiences, and how to get the best of it.

I

THE LONELINESS OF PLACE AND STATE

By the loneliness of state I mean the absence of

friends and intimate relationships in life. In that respect some of the noisest and busiest and most inhabited places may be the loneliest.

> "There is a loneliness that I have known
>   In walking through the crowded city street;
> I think that I have never been alone
>   Until I heard the measured cadence beat
> Of tramping feet set marching endlessly
> Along the agonizing thoroughfare." [1]

How true that is, that the greatest city in the world, with the most numerous population, may be the loneliest place on earth to him who is a stranger in its midst. I remember once visiting the mountain home, on the South Mountain near Antietam, of one of the celebrated war correspondents of the Civil War. It is in a most lonely and remote part of those beautiful mountains. A friend of this man meeting him once hurrying through the railroad station in New York, asked him where he was going. He said, "I'm going down to the mountains in Maryland. It's too lonely here in New York." The lonely mountain home was not a lonely place to him, for he had intimate relationships there and friendly, neighborly fellowship with the natives. But in New York's rush and roar he was only a stranger.

If I were a composer, I should like to compose an anthem on the voice of the cry, of a great city.

[1] Author unknown.

In such an anthem there would be the note and chord of ambition and mounting desire; the major chord of hope and worship; the minor chord of guilt and sin and fear and sorrow; the penetrating note of pain; the low-sounding chord of despair; the strident piercing note of greed; the howl of hate. But no anthem of the city would be complete which did not have sounding through it the deep, diapason note of loneliness.

Man was made for man, and it is not meet for him to be alone. It has been well said that he who loves solitude—that is, permanent, unbroken solitude—must be either a beast or a god. Once in the mountains of Kentucky I stayed in a mountain home with a man and his wife who perhaps not for a half a century had been out of that little valley. Once, indeed, they told me, they had started westward with other neighbors to settle in the Blue Grass country; but they had not gone far when a longing came over them for their own people. As they put it in their mountain way, "We didn't like to be so far away from the graves of our kin."

How, then, can we get the best of this kind of loneliness, the loneliness of absence of friends? It is important to do so, because the spirit of loneliness unrelieved, and uncontrolled, has a tendency to paralyze the energies of life and reduce one's efficiency and one's usefulness in life. Loneliness, too, especially the loneliness of a great city, if not dealt with, is likely to open dangerous gates and doors of temptation. There is no doubt that on the grave where many a man and women is buried—that is, the honorable and sacred part of them—the true inscription and epitaph might well be, "I was lonely." It is an important victory in life, then, to get the best of loneliness.

One way to do it is by the spirit of friendliness. It was said a long time ago, but still it is true, "He that would have friends must show himself friendly." The kindly, warm outlook toward other lives opens the way for pleasant, human relationships. One of the best and most natural and most approved methods of dealing with loneliness in a great city is association with a Christian church; and still better, active participation with the work and worship of the church, for this brings wholesome social contacts and friendships. I think one of the deepest satisfactions of ministers of wide experience will be the testimony which they receive through the years from those who found escape from loneliness in the friendly atmosphere of the church. Some of them will be those who have come in and have taken an active part in the work of the church, and who are well known to the minister; others whom he hardly knows at all, perhaps would not know them if he had met them on the street, but who slipped quietly into their pew at the morning or evening service, and in the worship of God's house and in the meditations of the preacher had their hearts warmed and their faith in God and in man established.

One should always try, too, to find some way in which to be a blessing to someone else. What we do for others not only cheers us and meets us at the end of life's journey, but cheers us and meets us now. A good motto for life is that which God gave to Abraham, "Be thou a blessing." That is a good thing to say to yourself when you wake up in the morning. No matter how you feel, you will feel better when you realize that it is possible for you to be a blessing to someone else. Let then the golden finger of the morning write those words as a motto across the wall of your room, whether it be in a spacious home, or in a hotel, or at the Y. M. C. A., or the Y. W. C. A., or a little cabined third-story-back room, "Be thou a blessing."

II

THE LONELINESS OF SORROW

There is no doubt about that kind of loneliness. So many who have been bereft of their friends have said to me that the hard thing to bear was the loneliness of it. We say, then, to our faith, "Hast thou a medicine for this kind of loneliness?"

GETTING THE BEST OF LONELINESS

"Joy is a partnership,
Grief weeps alone;
Many guests had Cana,
Gethsemane had one." [1]

One way to get the best of this kind of loneliness is not to cling to our sorrow, and, in a sense, worship it. Many do that to their own great hurt, to the dishonor of their Christian faith. Such grief serves no purpose and is no tribute to the departed friends. One who recently passed through great sorrow said to me that she felt keenly the loneliness of it, but that she was determined that she would turn this sorrow, the death of her mother, to some useful purpose in her own life and in the lives of others. Indeed, she said that had been one of the last messages of her mother, that when she was gone and the daughter no longer needed to care for her, she could go out and do good in the world, the good that the sick mother longed to do. The soul can find solace in Christian fellowship and in kind deeds for others. Margaret Ogilvy, in that beautiful tribute of a famous son to his mother, was one to whom all the women in the village went in their time of trouble and of sorrow. The son used to wonder at it, and then he remembered the great sorrow that had come into his mother's life in the death of her first born,

[1] Frederic Lawrence Knowles, in *More Heart Throbs*. Published by Grosset and Dunlap.

and he understood how it was there that she got her soft voice and tender ways.

It is always a good thing to think of the sorrow of others. In the famous poem of *The Bridge*, a man whose heart was hot and restless, and who thought to end his life and went out on the parapet of the bridge to do so, hearing the clock in the steeple strike the hour, began to think of the great number of burdened and sorrowing souls who had passed over that bridge before him, and as he thought of the sorrows of others the burden of his own sorrow fell from him.

> "But now it has fallen from me,
> It is buried in the sea;
> And only the sorrow of others
> Throws its shadow over me."

In the time of sorrow let us fall back upon the friendship of God. We often use those words, "Thou God seest me," as words to warn ourselves and others from temptation and sin, meaning that even if no one else sees or knows, God always sees us. All that is true; but that is not the way in which those words were first used. The handmaiden of Abraham, Hagar, had been driven out from Abraham's home by the jealousy and anger of the barren Sarah. The unfortunate girl lay there in despair in a lonely place in the wilderness. But it was there that the angel of the Lord came to speak to her and to comfort her and cheer her, and to tell her of the coming birth of Ishmael. So moved and so grateful was Hagar, that she called the name of that place where God spake to her, "Thou God seest me." "For," she said, "I also here looked after Him that seeth me." And the well by which she was resting when the angel appeared unto her was called, "Beer-lahai-roi," which means, "the well of the Living One who seeth me." Never forget that in the desert of your sorrow is the refreshing well of the presence and comfort of God. "Thou God seeth me."

III
THE LONELINESS OF TEMPTATION

This is one of the most powerful and most dangerous kinds of loneliness. Our Saviour knew what that kind of loneliness was. When He was tempted of the devil He was alone in the wilderness. And again at Gethsemane He left the eight disciples near the entrance, and took the remaining three, Peter and James and John, a little farther with Him into the garden; and then separated Himself from even them by the distance of a stone's cast, and there entered into His agony and trial.

The experience of temptation is one that we cannot share with others. There is always a stone's cast between the soul and even the nearest and the dearest friend when we enter the Garden of Temptation. There may be warnings and prayers and sympathy and solicitude, but when the hour of battle strikes we fight alone. We are as solitary as Christ was when Satan assailed Him in the wilderness. It makes no difference where the scene of the temptation is. It may be a busy office, a remote study, a crowded thoroughfare on the street, or a lonely country lane, but always the name of that place is Desert.

We have the Divine recipe and the Divine example as to how to get the best of temptation, and that is, by Watching and by Prayer. That was the method of Christ. He lived the upright, devoted life, and in the ordinary moments of that life—if indeed one might dare to say there were ordinary moments in the life of Christ—by His fidelity and faith He prepared for the great crises of His life when Satan assailed Him. Christ offers you that same sacred sword, your Excalibur and His, with which, by obedience to God and by strong and earnest prayer, we get the victory over temptation.

But what about those who have failed to get the victory over temptation, have not availed themselves of the spiritual weapons which were at their command, and, conquered by temptation, have fallen into sin? Ah! there is the deepest and darkest kind of loneliness. That was the loneliness that Peter knew when, having cursed his Lord, in a moment of weakness and cowardice, he heard the cock crow and went out into the night and wept bitterly. That was the kind of loneliness that Judas knew when, having received the sop, he went immediately out and "it was night," that dark and lonely night of sin.

How can the soul get the best of that kind of loneliness? In only one way—by repentance, by returning to God, and by receiving His forgiveness. How the loving voice of Christ sounds out through the dark and lonely night of sin, calling the sinner back to Him! "Let the wicked forsake his way, and the unrighteous man his thoughts: and let him return unto the Lord, and He will have mercy upon him; and to our God, for He will abundantly pardon."

The final penalty upon sin is unbroken loneliness, separation of our soul from God. But Christ on the Cross tasted that cup of bitterness and separation for you and me when He cried out, "My God, My God, why hast Thou forsaken Me!" He passed out into that awful loneliness, that you and I might never enter its eternal gloom. The one loneliness to fear and to dread is the loneliness of sin, and for that there is the great remedy of repentance and forgiveness.

There is, too, a noble loneliness of the soul, the loneliness that sometimes comes in the path of duty, the loneliness that comes as a price of conviction, the loneliness of dissent from what is sinful. I imagine that Vashti, the Queen of Ahasuerus, was lonely after she had been deposed from her high office and separated from the Persian Court because she refused to expose herself on the night of that drunken banquet, when Ahasuerus entertained a thousand of his lords. But it was a queenly and honorable and immortal loneliness, because it was the loneliness which was the price of honor and of self-respect. Far better to be lonely with a good conscience than to be in gay company with a bad conscience.

Everybody has some kind of a burden. Loneliness may be your burden—the one that God has chosen for you. It is a part of your discipline and probation in life. Therefore, do not complain about it, but bear it with courage and patience and fortitude. Remember, too, that you are not the only lonely person that has passed through this world. Some of the greatest benefactors of mankind have been lonely men, and Christ Himself was the Man of Sorrows, the Man who said, "I have trod the winepress alone."

It was Christ, too, who said, "And yet I am not alone, because the Father is with Me." He came that we might realize to the full the friendship of God. It was said of Abraham of old that he was the Friend of God. What was true of Abraham and of David, of John and of Paul, through Jesus Christ can be true of you. You, too, can be the friend of God. And where the friendship of God is, there we can pass through every lonely valley and drink every appointed cup. What a Friend we have in Jesus!

IX

GETTING THE BEST OF OUR ENEMIES

"They hanged Haman on the gallows that he had prepared for Mordecai"

Esther 7:10

"And he comforted them, and spake kindly unto them"

Genesis 50:21

THERE you have two ways of dealing with your enemies—the wrong way, the way that Haman took toward Mordecai; the right way, the way that Joseph took toward his brethren who had sold him into slavery. Let us look, first at the wrong way, or, How *not* to get the best of our enemies.

I

THE WRONG WAY

Haman built a gallows fifty cubits high on which to hang his enemy, Mordecai. In the early morning light, passersby in the city of Shushan saw a body dangling from a gallows fifty cubits high, and the vultures already circling around it. But it was not the body of Mordecai, for whom Haman had built the gallows, but the body of Haman himself. He was a victim of hate and revenge—not another's, but his own. A dismal and terrible sight, that body dangling there with the vultures wheeling around it. Yet it is not without profit that you pause to look upon this sight; for since every soul can hate, every man has in him the making of a Haman.

Haman was one of the chief ministers and satraps of the Persian despot, Ahasuerus. By native ability and shrewdness, although a foreigner, he had risen to the second place in the Persian empire. As the viceroy of Xerxes, everyone bowed and saluted when Haman passed by. But there was one who did not: Mordecai, the Jew. What lay back of this detestation by Mordecai of Haman, we do not know. Perhaps there had been some quarrel or feud in the past, for both men had posts at the court. What we do know is that Haman was not worthy of veneration or honor.

When Haman saw that when he left the palace Mordecai did not bow down before him, he was filled with rage and indignation. He told his wife that all the honors and wealth that the king had heaped upon him were as nothing to him so long as he saw that Jew refusing to do him honor. The more he brooded over it, the more possessed he was of an insane hatred and a wild thirst for revenge. Never did a man plan such a terrible revenge! It was not only the destruction of Mordecai that Haman planned and plotted, but the destruction of the whole race of the Jews!

This terrible revenge of Haman would have been accomplished, for he had persuaded the king to sign and seal the edict for the destruction of the Jews throughout the empire, had not God intervened, as He so frequently has done in the history of the world, in behalf of His people. This intervention was through two channels or agencies. First of all, the sleepless night of the Persian despot, who, unable to sleep, had his secretaries read him the records of the realm, and in the reading learned that Mordecai had saved his life on one occasion from assassination. The next morning the king summoned Haman and asked what should be done to the man whom the king delighted to honor. Confident that that man was himself, Haman suggested that a crown be put on his head, that he be arrayed in royal garments and mounted on a royal charger, and led through the streets of the city by one of the most noble princes of the realm, with a proclamation shouted by criers, "Thus shall it be done unto the man whom the king delighteth to honor!" Alas for Haman! For Xerxes told him that Mordecai was the man he delighted to honor, and the humiliated and crestfallen Haman was compelled to lead his enemy in triumph through the streets and avenues of the city.

That was bad enough, but worse was yet to come.

Through the intercession of the beautiful Queen Esther, successor to the noble Vashti, and adopted daughter and niece of Mordecai, Ahasuerus was persuaded to execute vengeance upon the cruel man who had plotted for the destruction of Israel. Haman was seized, hurried to the gallows, and hanged fifty cubits high.

Haman was a victim of his own hate. He was hanged on the gallows that he had arranged for another. He is the supreme egotist of the Bible, and love of self is the fountain of hatred. Hatred of another is only the shadow of love for yourself.

Haman is an illustration of the folly of permitting one thing to cloud our life. He had the respect, at least of the reverence and adulation, of everybody in Persia; all except one man Mordecai. Fool that he was, he let that one exception cloud and darken and distort his whole life. From India to Greece, and from the Caspian Sea to the Arabian sands, there was not a palace, nor a treasure, a jewel, a garment, a tree, a woman, a town, that Haman could not have had for the asking. But when he saw one humble Jew refusing to do him honor, that spoiled it all. He forgot everything that he had and centered his mind on the one thing that he could not have.

That has been typical of human nature from the beginning. Our first parents were not satisfied with the abundance and beauty of the Garden in which they had been placed, and centered their attention, not on the many trees of which they could eat, but on the one tree of which they could not eat. And it was that one tree that blasted the happiness of the Garden for them. Center your thought on the things that you have, not on the things that you cannot have. Center your thought on the friends you have, who love you and respect you, and do not let your mind dwell upon the others. Haman would have been a wise man, instead of a wicked fool, had he said to himself, "Mordecai evidently does not think much of me. But there are a great many who do, and I shall not permit one man to spoil all the rest for me. After all, the world is big enough for both me and Mordecai."

Aaron Burr is an instance of a gifted and able man who permitted hatred to get the best of him. When he and Jefferson were deadlocked in the House of Representatives for the presidency, it was the influence of Alexander Hamilton, who likened Burr to Cataline, that led to his defeat for the presidency. Again, in 1804 it was the influence of Hamilton, who wrote the letters disparaging the character of Burr, that played a prominent part in Burr's defeat for the governorship of New York. After these two overthrows, Burr was possessed of hatred toward Hamilton and killed him in the fatal duel on the tragic shores of Weehawken. But the pistol shot which took the life of Hamilton also took the political life and the national reputation of Aaron Burr. Long afterwards, he confessed that it would have been wiser for him had he taken the sensible view that the world was big enough for both Aaron Burr and Alexander Hamilton.

It was bad enough for Haman to permit one thing to spoil the happiness of his life, but still worse for him to permit the disrespect of Mordecai to fill his heart with an all-consuming hatred. That is always the danger of hatred; it opens the door to transgression and to sin. And when a man has had his revenge, as he calls it, he discovers that the one who is most injured is himself, just as Haman did when they hanged him fifty cubits high on the gallows that he had built for Mordecai.

Hatred is the most fearful passion that can enter the human heart, and he who admits it has within him, potentially, all crime and wickedness. That was why Christ said, "Whosoever is angry with his brother without cause shall be in danger of the judgment." And "that disciple whom Jesus loved," and who leaned upon His breast at the Supper, knew the devastating power of hatred, when he said "Whosoever hateth his brother is in darkness."

Everyone ought to dig a grave, deep within his own heart, where he buries far out of sight the injuries and hatreds and enmities of life. Jules Verne in his

Twenty Thousand Leagues Under the Sea was the prophet of the submarine, with its cruel devastation and destruction. Possessed with hatred of mankind, Captain Nemo ranges the seas in his submarine, the "Nautilus," and takes fearful and titanic vengeance upon the human race. The book comes to a close with the description of the sinking of a man-of-war, and the swarm of seamen, like a human ant heap overtaken by the sea, struggling in the waters and clinging to the hull of the sinking ship, until the dark mass disappeared and was sucked down into the depths. A seaman, a prisoner on the "Nautilus," viewing the tragedy, turned to look at Captain Nemo: "I turned to Captain Nemo. That terrible avenger, a perfect archangel of hatred, was still looking. When all was over, he turned to his room, opened the door, and entered. I followed him with my eyes. On the end wall, beneath his heroes, I saw the portrait of a woman still young, and two little children. Captain Nemo looked at them for some moments, stretched his arms toward them, and kneeling down burst into deep sobs." Then he heard the Captain exclaim, "Almighty God! Enough! Enough!" And with that the "Nautilus" was sucked down into the whirlpool of the maelstrom. The anguish and solitude of Captain Nemo are a powerful parable of the wages of hatred, and what happens to a man when he tries to get the best of his enemies by hating them and destroying them.

II

THE RIGHT WAY

If Haman is the ugliest character in the Bible, Joseph is the most beautiful, the most Christlike. His story is the greatest story of all time. The boy of many dreams, with the coat of many colors, hated by his jealous brothers, was sold for a slave to the Midianites who carried him down into Egypt. There, in the household of Potiphar, a worse fate befell Joseph. Falsely accused of a hideous crime, he was committed to prison, where he spent long and weary years.

But at length the Daystar of Hope rose over his dungeon. Joseph, remembered by the ungrateful chief butler, whose dream he had interpreted, but who had forgotten him for so long a time, is delivered from the dungeon to interpret the dreams of Pharaoh. Now the tide turns in the life of Joseph. Where before everything had gone against him, now everything is in his favor. He is exalted to the second place in Pharaoh's empire, and wears Pharaoh's gold chain about his neck. Happily married, he names one of his children Manasseh: "For God," he said, "hath made me to forget all my toil and all my father's house." And the name of the second he called Ephraim: "For God has caused me to be fruit-

ful in the land of my affliction." But when Joseph
named his firstborn Manasseh, all that he meant was
that he had forgotten the bitterness and darkness
of the past. He did not mean that he had forgotten
his father, or his brethren. No, Joseph could never
do that! Often his wife, as she sat with him at the
table, or the lords of Pharaoh when they came to
consult him on business, wondered at the far-away
look of strange abstraction in Joseph's eyes. He was
thinking not about Egypt and its splendors, but the
black tents at Hebron, and Jacob, his father, who had
made him the coat of many colors, and his brothers,
even although they had treated him so harshly—
Judah and Simeon, and Levi, and the rest of them,
and dearest of all, his own full brother, Benjamin.

One day Joseph was told that Hebrews from
Canaan had come down to buy corn. When the ten
men were ushered into his presence, Joseph knew
them immediately. The years vanished in a moment.
But they did not know Joseph in his high estate and
royal robes. For a time Joseph dealt severely with
them and spoke roughly to them, and sent them back,
retaining Simeon as a hostage, and charged them with
stealing his silver cup. And then on a second visit
he demanded that they leave Benjamin as a hostage.
All this, perhaps, was to awaken remorse within the
hearts of those cruel brothers. And indeed, although
they were not certain who Joseph was, that was

exactly what happened; for when Joseph made the demand of them that they bring their youngest brother down with them, they said one to another, "We are verily guilty concerning our brother in that we saw the anguish of his soul when he besought us, and we would not hear. Therefore is this distress come upon us."

Having stirred their conscience, Joseph, no longer able to disguise himself and disguise his heart, has all strangers and foreigners go out from his chambers and then discloses himself unto his brothers. "I am Joseph! Doth my father yet live?" When his brothers heard that, they were silent, for they were terrified. Now Joseph would take vengeance and kill them all! But instead of that, Joseph called them to him and said, "I am Joseph your brother, whom ye sold into Egypt. Now therefore be not grieved, nor angry with yourselves, that ye sold me hither: for God send me before you to preserve life. . . . So now it was not you that sent me hither, but God. . . . As for you, ye thought evil against me; but God meant it unto good, to save much people alive. Now therefore fear ye not: I will nourish you, and your little ones. And he comforted them, and spake kindly unto them."

Marvelous scene! A beautiful triumph of forgiveness! Joseph was a great Christian before Christ came. When we speak of the "Christian spirit," what do we mean? We mean the forgiving spirit. And in all the Bible, Joseph, after Christ Himself, is the most beautiful example of the forgiving spirit. His was a triumph, not only of love and affection, but of faith in the providence of God. He looked back over that hard road that he had taken, over that dark and painful past, and now saw how all the time God had been leading him. His brothers had hated him and envied him and sold him into Egypt, and wicked, licentious Potiphar's wife had tempted him and accused him, and Potiphar had cast him into the dungeon, and the chief butler had forgotten him. But God was in it all, because through the influence that he had now as prime minister of Pharaoh, Joseph was able to save the lives of his father and his brethren and all their people from starvation. "God meant it unto good." That is a real triumph of faith, if in some of the most painful experiences of life you can see that God's hand was upon you and leading you. It was the fine thought of Pascal that Christ called the traitor, Judas, "friend"—because, even in his wickedness and betrayal, Judas was the agent of the will of God.

Here, then, are the two ways of dealing with your enemies. There is the way of Haman—to hate your enemy and wish him ill and seek to do him ill. The end of that way is misery and unhappiness. Hannah More used to say that if she had a bitter enemy, and wished to punish him, she would teach him to hate someone. If you wish to punish yourself, hate someone else in life. The other way was the way of Joseph—the way of forgiveness and reconciliation. That, too, was the way of Christ, who not only taught us to forgive one another, but who Himself practiced it, and when they were nailing Him to the cruel Cross, prayed, "Father, forgive them; for they know not what they do."

As a child I used to hear that verse read from the book of Proverbs, and repeated also by St. Paul in his letter to the Romans, "If thine enemy hunger, feed him; if he thirst, give him drink: for in so doing thou heap coals of fire on his head," and wondered just what it meant. I saw a picture of a man with a coal scuttle full of burning coal taking the shovel and shoveling the coals on the head of his enemy. But how did that fit in with feeding him, and giving him to drink? The wisest commentators today seem to know no more about that verse than did the child with his childish vision of the coal shovel and the scuttle. But whatever it means, it tells us that we get revenge upon our enemies by loving them, and not by hating them, by doing them good, and not evil.

When Washington's army was stationed near Philadelphia, a soldier in the army, a wicked and disloyal man, was court-martialed and sentenced to be hanged. On the day set for his execution there appeared at Washington's headquarters a godly Quaker who lived at Ephrata. He had gone on foot all the distance from Ephrata to Philadelphia to plead for the life of the condemned man. Washington heard his plea, and then said to him that he was sorry, but he could do nothing to stay the execution of the sentence. The condemned man was a notorious violator of the law and must reap the due reward of his deeds. Then, as he turned to leave, Washington said to the Quaker, "Are you a relative of the man?" "No," answered the Quaker. "Are you his friend, then?" said Washington. "No," said the Quaker, "he was my deadly enemy."

X

GETTING THE BEST OF MARRIAGE

*"The head of the woman is the man.
. . . But the woman is the glory of the
man. . . . Neither is the man without
the woman, neither the woman without the man, in the Lord"*

I Corinthians 11:3,7,11

THE ascertainable facts
show that marriage gets the best of about one out of
every five couples who enter its territory. This
is only the legal record, and no doubt the number
of those over whom marriage gets the best is much
higher. From available statistics, the indications are
that for the thirteen years commencing with 1928
and going through 1940, in the neighborhood of three
million marriages will have been dissolved by the
courts. This means six million separated husbands
and wives; and estimating two children to a family,
it means that there are six million children in these
broken homes, or a total population in the United
States, during thirteen years only, of twelve million
persons who have been affected in one way or another
by the failure of marriage.

These statistics are sufficient to show the importance of my subject, "Getting the Best of Marriage,"

for the number of those over whom marriage gets the best is truly appalling.

There are those, indeed, who look upon such statistics as these with great satisfaction. To them it is a sign of progress, and of the emancipation of men and women, especially women, from the superstitions and rigid customs of the past. But the logic and mathematics of history are all on the other side of the argument. Whether we go to little Judea, or to ancient Rome, the breakdown of marriage and the thawing out of family morality have been the symptoms and the forerunners of national decline, deterioration, and death. Indeed, hearing facts such as these which I have just quoted, raises the question, Is America on the road to ruin? Is America taking the same path that the nations of the past followed when they went down to ruin and destruction? While we discuss eagerly international questions and domestic problems, and are engrossed with such subjects as education and taxation and industry and finance, all the time this terrible cancer, the corruption of the home, grows and swells and spreads in the national breast.

What is the chief cause for marriage getting the best of so many married people, so that here in supposedly Christian America the number of marriages per one thousand which end in shipwreck has increased from 62 in 1890 to 175 in 1937? Undoubtedly, the chief cause is the general abandonment of the Christian view of marriage. According to this Scriptural and Christian conception, marriage is holy. As our Presbyterian wedding service puts it, "We are assembled here in the presence of God to join this man and this woman in holy marriage, which is instituted of God, regulated by His commandments, blessed by our Lord Jesus Christ, and to be held in honor among all men. Let us, therefore, reverently remember how God hath blessed and sanctified marriage for the welfare and happiness of mankind."

According to this noble statement, marriage is a divine institution. Protestants do not hold it to be one of the sacraments, as do the Roman Catholics; but we believe that it is highly sacred, instituted of God, and regulated by His commandments. When the first marriage took place and the first husband called the first wife Woman, the record is, "Therefore shall a man leave his father and his mother, and shall cleave unto his wife: and they shall be one flesh." Ages afterwards, when that fine custom had been corrupted among the Jews, as among all other peoples— one man living in honor and affection with one woman —the Pharisees came to Jesus and asked Him if it was lawful for a man to put away his wife for every, that is, any, cause? Jesus referred them to the laws of Moses and the indulgence that these laws gave to man's nature and hardness of heart. He then carried them back to the Divine plan and charter of marriage, saying that from the beginning it was not so, and that "from the beginning of the creation God made them male and female." Then He quoted the verse from Genesis, "For this cause shall a man leave his father and mother, and cleave to his wife; and they twain shall be one flesh; so then they are no more twain, but one flesh." And then Christ makes His own great addendum, echoed at so many marriage services, "What therefore God hath joined together, let no man put asunder."

This is the Christian idea of marriage, very beautiful and very high. The departure from it on the part of so many thousands, and on the part of our own nation, is due not only to the natural inclinations of our fallen human nature, what Christ refers to as the "hardness of our hearts," but to a now long-time systematic teaching of what we might call the brute theory of man's origin and the development of his social life and custom. This, in reality, although often glossed and varnished, leaves no place for God, or His commandments, and banishes completely the beautiful Christian conception of marriage. It is the non-recognition, then, of the law of God with regard to marriage which is the fundamental cause for the fact that marriage, which was devised and instituted of God for the welfare and happiness of mankind, in so many cases, instead of bringing men happiness and establishing their welfare, gets the best of mankind and brings them unhappiness and disrupts their life.

But, it will be pointed out, there are many thousands who have not formally abandoned the Scriptural and Christian ideal of marriage. They have Christian background and training, to a degree, and they enter into marriage with the beautiful ceremony of the Christian Church. And yet marriage gets the best of great numbers of them also. How shall we account for this?

One reason is what we might call the lack of the "mind set." A Pittsburgh judge sometime ago, after commenting on the wholesale perjury which prevailed in the testimony given in the majority of cases of broken homes which came into his court, made the observation that the old idea that when a man and a woman were married it was "till death do us part," seems to have been generally abandoned. We hear that solemn, and yet very beautiful, phrase at the marriage ceremony, "Till death do us part"; but in view of what has taken place in the world, we cannot but ask ourselves, when that phrase echoes in our mind, How far short of death will this relationship be dissolved? Young people know that thousands upon thousands have in one way or another cast off the bonds of marriage, and in the back of their mind, no doubt, is the idea that they can do likewise, should occasion or desire arise.

Another reason for marriage getting the best of so many people, is that so many who enter into it regard it just as an expedition of pleasure or convenience. The phrase, "in the bonds of Holy Marriage," is very significant. The "bonds" may be silken and scented with rosewater; nevertheless, they are real bonds, and the failure to recognize that fact explains the shipwreck of many a marriage. When marriage is entered into lightly and carelessly instead of "soberly, advisedly, and in the fear of God," little thought is given to the "bonds" of marriage; and when not only plenty, but want comes, not only joy but sorrow, not only health but sickness, then the temptation is to break these bonds asunder; for not duty, but pleasure, is the chief consideration. Paul's searching description of the society of his day tells, after all, the real story of the breakdown and corruption of human society today—Men are "lovers of pleasures more than lovers of God."

Lack of sufficient acquaintance before marriage is another reason for the victory that marriage gets over so many persons. There is something in the saying, "Love at first sight and divorce at the first fight." The lack of a solid economic basis, too, leads to great distress in the marriage relationship, and frequently to its dissolution. Twenty-five dollars a week income and twenty-four dollars a week expenditures is heaven, whereas twenty-five dollars a week income and twenty-six dollars a week expenses is hell. Debt, living beyond one's income, spells the doom of many a marriage. Eve was the first woman who was not content to live within her income, and disastrous results ensued.

A bad temper, an unpleasant disposition, can destroy the joy and happiness of marriage and dissolve marriage itself. A man quite aged went once to his physician for a physical examination. The physician expressed astonishment at his robust vigor in spite of his advanced years. The man explained that he had been compelled to live an "out-of-doors life." He then went on to say that when he and his wife were married they made a compact that when he lost his temper she was to keep silence, and when she lost her temper he was to go out of doors. A sudden flash and flame of anger can wither the flowers in the fairest Paradise of any earthly home.

There is a tradition that Jonathan Edwards, third president of Princeton and America's greatest thinker, had a daughter with an ungovernable temper. But, as is so often the case, this infirmity was not known to the outside world. A worthy young man fell in love with this daughter and sought her hand in marriage. "You can't have her," was the abrupt answer of Jonathan Edwards. "But I love her," the young man replied. "You can't have her," said Edwards. "But she loves me," replied the young man. Again Edwards said, "You can't have her." "Why?" said the young man. "Because she is not worthy of you." "But," he asked, "she is a Christian, is she not?" "Yes, she is a Christian, but the grace of God can live with some people with whom no one else could ever live."

Still another chief cause for the failure of so many people to get the best of marriage is a lack of Christian kindness and gentleness and tenderness. So far as the causes given in the courts for unhappiness in marriage, and grounds upon which marriages are dissolved, are concerned, "cruel and barbarous treatment" always stands first, in a class by itself. Of course, it is well known that that is often just a blind, a false front, which either covers more serious offenses, or is merely a pretext on the part of those who desire to be separated. "Cruel and barbarous treatment" can cover anything from wearing suspenders to actual infidelity. Nevertheless, not in this false and hypocritical sense of the divorce courts, but *real* cruelty, *real* lack of Christian kindness and Christian tenderness spells the doom of many a marriage. Sometimes people take exception to the injunction of St. Paul to wives, that they "submit themselves unto their husbands," and to Peter's, "Wives, be in subjection to your own husbands." But those who do so seem to have forgotten what kind of husbands these are about whom the apostles speak, and for whom they ask this recognition and honor. What kind of husbands are they? It is the husband who "loves his wife, even as Christ also loved the Church and gave Himself for it"; beautiful, unchanging, sacrificial love. And again, as Peter puts it, the husbands who "dwell with their wives, and give honor unto the wife, as unto the weaker vessel, as being heirs together of the grace of life." How beautiful that is, "Heirs together of the grace of life!"

Underlying all these reasons which I have just given for defeat in the marriage relationship is the fundamental cause, and that is the lack of God in the lives of men and women, and hence the lack of reverence, the lack of patience, the lack of tenderness and kindness, and the lack of faith. Homes that are consecrated to God with a Family Altar rarely suffer shipwreck. I have never yet come across one that did.

Having spoken of broken marriages, and the reasons why they are broken, now, in conclusion, let me speak of the unbroken, abiding, "until-death-do-us-part" marriages. And how many of these, thank God, there still are! They do not get into the newspapers. They are not featured in the society columns; yet these are the marriages and these are the homes which are the fountain source whence flow the streams of blessing and inspiration for our national life. Where husbands and wives dwell together, honoring and respecting one another, and where they bring up their children in the nurture and admonition of the Lord, there is the strength and there the hope of the Church and of the nation. One can suffer and sorrow, and pass through hardship alone; but for happiness two are required. Leigh Hunt speaks in beautiful music of the two homes which are possible for man, the happy Christian home in this world and the home "beyond the stars":

> "For there are two heavens sweet,
>   Both made of love—one inconceivable
> Even by the other, so divine it is;
> The other far on this side of the stars,
>   By men called home."

There are, indeed, those two heavens which are made of love. One lies beyond the stars. We cannot behold it, although we hope one day to enter into it. The other lies, "far on this side of the stars." It is the Christian home.

> "As long as there are homes to which men turn
>   At the close of day,
> So long as there are homes where children are,
>   Where women stay,
> If love and loyalty and faith be found
>   Across those sills,
> A stricken nation can recover
>   From those ills."

XI

GETTING THE BEST OF JEALOUSY

*"Jealousy is as cruel as the grave: the
coals thereof are coals of fire"*

Song of Solomon 8:6

ONE of the pleasant
memories of my boyhood days is of a visit that we
used to make, my brother and I, about once every
year to a farm that lay across the Ohio River. We
would take the train down the river to another town,
and there cross the river on a ferryboat. And what
an adventure that was! They who cross the ocean for
the first time get no greater thrill out of that first
crossing than we did out of that ride on the ferryboat across the river. Then through the cool and
beautiful glen for a mile or two; then the winding
road up the side of the hills, until we came to the
farmhouse. There everything in its humble sim-
plicity aroused our interest and enthusiasm, from the
livestock at the farmyard to the gastronomic triumphs of the kitchen and the pantry.

There were two dogs on the farm, "Shep" and
"Brave," a fine shepherd, and a mongrel close-
skinned dog. They were boon companions and
roamed the forest together. Together they hunted
for groundhogs and rabbits, and together, with

melancholy and dejected mien, they trod the tread-mill of the dog-churn. The dogs were good friends; but if you put your hand down and patted one of them, immediately the bristles began to rise on the back of the other, and a warning growl proceeded from his jaws. You were fortunate if a fierce battle did not ensue. Jealousy! Its empire extends from the brute creation to man, the prince of creation.

In the Song of Solomon it is written, "Jealousy is as cruel as the grave. The coals thereof are the coals of fire." It is not Solomon, but a woman who is made to say that, and she ought to know. To understand the force of this comparison of jealousy and the grave, walk with me through the grassy aisles of the cemetery, and in musing meditation read the names and the dates that are graven on the tombs. Here is the grave of a man who lived to be almost a hundred years old; and here the grave of him who died at the Psalmist's allotted span, threescore and ten; and there the grave of one who died in middle life; and here the grave of a young man, and yonder the tomb of an infant who "did but yesterday suspire." The grave lays its exactions upon all ages, all periods of mortal life. These brief inscriptions tell the story of the life that here was rounded in a sleep. Some were men and some were women; some were poor and some were rich; some were ignorant and some were learned; some were unknown and some were well known; some were vicious, perhaps criminal, and some were Christlike and saintly in their lives; some died believing in Jesus and in hope of a blessed resurrection, and some died without faith and without hope. Thus we see that the grave takes in all classes and conditions. The cemetery is a cross section of humanity. Now we begin to see the truth and power of the comparison of jealousy and the grave, for, like the grave, jealousy preys upon all ages and sexes and kinds and conditions of men. Jealousy is as cruel as the grave!

Nor is the second comparison of the text any the less forceful. "The coals thereof are coals of fire, which hath a most vehement flame." Many and fierce are the flames which leap out of the furnace of the heart of man. Vehement is the flame of lust, or hate, or pride, or scorn, or anger, or revenge; but most vehement of all, scorching unto death every good thing that comes within its path, is the flame of jealousy.

The first crime that stained the history of the race was committed by a jealous man. "And Abel was a keeper of sheep, but Cain was a tiller of the ground. And it came to pass in process of time that Cain brought of the fruit of the ground an offering unto the Lord. And Abel, he also brought the firstlings of the flock. And the Lord had respect unto Abel and to his offerings; but unto Cain and to his offering he had not respect. And Cain was very wroth, and his countenance fell at the saying. And it came to pass, when they were in the field, that Cain rose up against Abel his brother, and slew him." The first inhumanity of man to man was wrought by jealousy. The first blow that man ever struck against man was the blow of a jealous man. Alas! how many crimes since then it has committed; what eminent careers it has wrecked; what good causes it has hindered; what nations it has drenched with blood; what cities it has consumed with fire; what hopes it has blasted; what hearts it has broken, and what homes it has blighted with its withering curse. Yes, jealousy is as cruel as the grave; the coals thereof are coals of fire, which hath a most vehement flame.

I

JEALOUSY AMONG RACES AND NATIONS

The spade of the archaeologist digging beneath the site of Roman Carthage has opened up to our investigation the ruins of ancient Carthage. The great Phoenician city was destroyed by the Roman armies in 146 B.C., the last chapter in the long and bitter contest with Rome, which had raged intermittently for one hundred and twenty-two years. When Porcius Cato returned from an embassy to Carthage after the Second Punic War, he was so impressed with the surviving greatness of the African metropolis, that thereafter he never finished any speech in the Senate without sounding the warning, "Carthage must be destroyed." The feud between Carthage and Rome ravished that part of the world with fire and sword and stained the seas with blood. When the Romans finally took the city, all the buildings were leveled to the ground, and the site was dedicated with the most solemn imprecations to the infernal gods, and all human habitation throughout the vast ruined area was expressly forbidden. Today the thick bed of cinders, blackened stones, broken glass, fragments of metal twisted by fire and half calcined bones found under the site of Roman Carthage bear grim witness to the appalling fate which overtook the city, and to the consuming, cursing, and destroying influence of jealously between the nations.

The flaming torch of jealousy is a light which helps you to read and understand the pages of human history. A few years before the last great war, a distinguished Scottish preacher wrote these words: "We all deplore the fact that Europe is an armed camp, and tremble lest the signal of war be given. What is the influence which maintains this intolerable bondage and may yet fling these masses of men at each other's throats? Whatever the politicians may say, it is not patriotism. The next great European war will not be an outburst of patriotism to cast off a yoke or to secure liberty for the slave; it will be a duel between nations inflamed and blinded by racial jealousy." The words were fearfully fulfilled. It was national jealousy which turned the sun into darkness and the moon into blood, and poured out the tears of mankind like an ocean. The dark history of the past will repeat itself unless good will and co-operation shall replace hate and jealousy as the principles for international relationships.

Again the world is darkened with the tragedy of two great nations, nations which have so much in common as to blood and religion, and ideals of life—the English and the German, engaged in a bitter war which will bring sorrow and destruction to untold millions. In one sense, this war is a war of international jealousy. One nation wants to take the other's place in the sun.

II

JEALOUSY BETWEEN INDIVIDUALS

The first case of jealousy in the world, and the source of the first crime, was the jealousy of the evil for the good. Cain slew Abel because his own works were evil and Abel's righteous. Goodness will always invite scorn and persecution on the part of evil. The accuser of his brethren is ever abroad. Satanic malignity is often called into action by purity of heart and meekness of life in another person. He who climbs high must look down on the hate and scorn of those below him. The eruption of evil passions which took place when Jesus appeared on earth is the crowning illustration of how purity of character, which we like to think will evoke all that is good in man and impel men to go and do likewise, ofttimes has the very opposite effect, and uncovers bottomless pits of wickedness in men, provoking them to the worst of crimes. Pilate perceived, says Mark, that for envy the chief priests had delivered up Jesus. Jealousy, which compassed the first murder, reached its awful climax when it delivered up Jesus to be crucified upon the cross.

In his Note Books, Leonardo da Vinci has a powerful passage on envy, which is the twin sister of jealousy. He says of envy: "She is made wounded by the sight of palm and olive. She is made wounded in the ear by laurel and myrtle, to signify that victory and truth offend her."

The quarrels and bitternesses among men of ability and education, statesmen, artists, musicians, scholars, and even clergymen, are too notorious to call for more than passing comment. Jealousy is the spur with which the devil will ride the noblest tempers. There are men of the finest parts, of splendid disposition and character in other areas of their life, but who cannot bear to hear another man praised, especially if that man's activities lie in the same field of endeavor.

One of the famous preachers of Scotland confessed to his brother ministers how many a Sabbath evening, after his younger colleague had preached to a greater throng in the evening than he did in the morning, he had gone home from the crowded church to chew the sheets in pain and chagrin at the greater success of his younger colleague. The passion of jealousy, hot and wild, knocked at the door of his heart, but he refused it admittance.

Jealousy was the rock upon which Saul made shipwreck of his life. His otherwise fine character was completely corrupted and perverted by the poison of jealousy. When the dancing women who went out to greet David after his victory over Goliath sang, "Saul hath slain his thousands, but David his tens of thousands," then jealousy was born in the heart of Saul. "And Saul eyed David from that day and forward"; and the eye through which he looked was green with envy and jealousy, now driving him to acts of maniacal fury, and now submerging him in the gulf of gloom and depression. That was the beginning of it, that day when Saul first heard the women praising David. The end of it was when Saul and his three sons lay dead upon the bloody slopes of Mount Gilboa.

One of the great artists stood one day before the work of a greater contemporary, one whose talents were far superior to his own. But instead of being depressed, or filled with envy or bitterness, he exclaimed, as he surveyed the beautiful work which expressed so fully ideas which he himself had not been able to realize, "I, too, am a painter!"

But there are few like him. Dean Swift puts the case fairly and squarely, and his satire is but little exaggeration over life, when he says in the "Lines on the Death of Dr. Swift":

> "We all behold with envious eyes
> Our equals raised above our size.
> Who would not at a crowded show
> Stand high himself, keep others low?
> I love my friend as well as you;
> But why should he obstruct my view?
>
> "What poet would not grieve to see
> His brothers write as well as he?
> But rather than they should excell
> Would wish his rivals all in hell?
> Her end when emulation misses,
> She turns to envy, stings and hisses;
> The strongest friendships yield to pride,
> Unless the odds be on our side.
> Vain humankind! Fantastic race!
> Thy various follies who can trace?
> Self-love, ambition, envy, pride,
> Their empire in our hearts divide."

These personal jealousies, which have embittered the relationships of individuals, have also done great injury to good causes. It is sad, but true, that the fine enthusiasm of a good cause does not overcome, as it ought, the selfishness of human nature. More than once the jealousy of generals prolonged the bitter contest of the Civil War, for when it came to the crisis there were men who placed their feelings and their rights above the great ends of justice.

In striking contrast with the jealousies which hindered the efforts of the leaders of the Northern armies, was the magnanimous and generous spirit displayed by General Robert E. Lee, commander of the Southern armies. After the Battle of Fair Oaks, or Seven Pines, the second battle on the Peninsula with McClellan's army, Joseph E. Johnston, the very able Confederate commander, was disabled by a fragment of a shell which struck him on the breast. The command immediately developed upon the next in rank, General W. H. Smith. But in the meantime, Jefferson Davis had appointed General Lee to take command of the army in the field. But Lee, before starting for the front, wrote a friendly note to General Smith, urging him to make an attack and win a victory before he himself could get to the front and take command.

III
JEALOUSY IN DOMESTIC LIFE

Here jealousy burns with its hottest and most devouring flame. The fire that sweeps over the prairie, leaving blackness and death behind it, is not so swift and terrible as the blistering blaze of jealousy. Here more than anywhere else we realize how cruel jealousy is and how terrible its flame. It is in this realm of love where man can reach his highest happiness that he also suffers his deepest misery and most acute anguish of soul, for jealousy is the "injured lover's hell." When love, which can lift man to the heights, begins to turn, or trembles for the object of its affections, it can cast man into the lowest hell. John Bunyan pictured the Celestial City with a door opening down into hell. So the heaven of domestic and personal and conjugal love has a door that opens down into the hell of jealousy.

When you land at Famagusta, near ancient Salamis, on the coast of Cyprus, where the apostle Paul, with Barnabas and John Mark, landed on his great enterprise so many centuries ago, you go to visit an ancient castle with deep moat, immense walls, and great circular towers. As you walk through the gloomy chambers of this ancient fortress and castle, the words of Shakespeare's *Othello* come to your mind, for this is the reputed site of that great tragedy of domestic jealousy, when the wicked Iago poisoned the mind of the distracted Moor and roused his wild jealousy against his beautiful and innocent wife, Desdemona.

Noble souls like Othello, once opening the door to jealousy, are metamorphosed into demons of hate and rage. The materials for Shakespeare's *Othello* could be supplied by many a private home in this city tonight, for jealousy and its cruel ravages are never

[143]

out of date. How often we see in the papers the account of some crime where the story commences with the words, "In a jealous rage." This worst of sins and passions is the worst of mockers. It fills its victim's heart with a wild craving and passionate desire and leads him to some lawless or wicked act, only to laugh at his calamity. He has struck the blow of jealousy, or carried out its hideous bidding in vituperation or slander, that worst murder of character, only to find that the blow has returned upon his own head, and that the fearful pangs of jealousy have not been quenched. Jealousy lures the soul on to a fierce banquet of hate, and then tortures and mocks it with hunger.

> "O beware of jealousy!
> It is the green-eyed monster that doth mock
> The meat it feeds upon."

Have you ever felt the flame of jealousy in your heart? Has that serpent ever hissed in your ear? Is there some one in your line of work or service whose name has brought a passing cloud over your face? Is there any one whose superior talents and gifts have made you secretly gnash your teeth? Is there any one whose beauty you secretly hate? Whose goodness you scorn? Is there under the sun a single person whose affection you fear might be turned, or is now turning, toward someone else? Then beware of jealousy. Stamp this flame out before the winds have fanned it into fury, and your happiness here and hereafter is destroyed.

The time to attack jealousy is when you feel the first sting of its scorching flame. I remember sitting once in the office of a physician and talking with him about a victim of cancer, then lying near death, the dread enemy having conquered portion after portion of the body. The doctor said, for the woman had come to him only after losing precious time and money on quack remedies, "If two years ago that woman had submitted to an operation, she would now be walking about and doing her work." But instead of that, soothing measures were taken and the virus spread through her system. Jealousy is like cancer. It must be dealt with in its incipient stage. When fully developed there is no surgery or medicine which can remove it.

Jealousy is the most awful sin, because there is no depth to which it will not descend, no serpentine subtlety of which it is not capable, no cruelty at which it will stop, and no character, however otherwise fine and strong, which it cannot, if once admitted, bring to ruin, and no garden of love and happiness which it cannot enter and destroy. Even the silent dead are not safe from its ravages.

St. Martin on a journey once fell in with two men and walked with them by the way. When he came to a parting of the road where he must leave them, he was so displeased with their selfish and envious natures that he said to them, "Before I go, I will bestow a boon upon you. Whatever you wish you shall have. But the man who wishes second will have twice as much as the man who makes the first wish." The two men, one a greedy man and the other an envious man, then walked along the road, each waiting for the other to wish first. The greedy man would not wish first, because he wanted to have twice as much as the other man, and the envious man would not wish first because he could not endure the thought of the other man having twice as much as he would have. At length the greedy man grew impatient and angry, and taking the envious man by the throat, began to choke him, and said to him, "You must wish, or I will kill you!" Whereupon the envious man said, "If it is a choice between death and making the first wish, then I will make the wish." And with a wicked look upon his eye, he said, "I wish that one of my eyes shall be blind." Immediately he lost the sight of one eye, and straightway the other, the greedy man, lost the sight of both eyes. A powerful parable of the self-destructive reaction of envy, jealousy, and greed.

Larger interests, good works, forgetting self and what is due to self, and trying to have the Christlike thought for others, this will be of great help in forfending jealousy from your soul. But if jealousy once gets a foothold in your life, or if its flames have commenced to burn within, then I know of but one remedy, and that is Christ. He, and He alone, can cast out this unclean spirit. Let Him in, that He may cast out the devil. There are some faults that you can restrain and that you can pray away and educate away. But jealousy is a sin that must be crucified. Crucify it! Christ talked about a devil that cometh not out save by fasting and prayer. This is certainly true of the hideous devil of jealousy. It cometh not out save by fasting and prayer. Crucify it!

XII

GETTING THE BEST OF DOUBT

"They worshiped him: but some doubted"

Matthew 28:17

So it has been from the very beginning. When He appeared to them on that mountaintop after His resurrection, and before His ascension into heaven, some worshiped Christ as God and Saviour, but some doubted Him. So it will be down to the very end. Man's great adversary and tempter sowed the seeds of doubt at the creation of man. He raised doubts as to the Word of God, as to whether what God said would come to pass. "Hath God said?"

When Christ appeared yonder on that mountain, some believed and some doubted. But the men who moved the world, who turned the world upside down, who set flowing streams of truth and influence which yet bless mankind, were not the men who doubted, but the men who believed.

The question of doubt is all important. Some people take the view that after all it makes little or no difference what a man believes. But that certainly was not the view of mankind's greatest Teacher, and the world's Redeemer, our Lord and Saviour Jesus Christ. At the end of the great Sermon on the

Mount, He told the story of the house that was built on the rock, and which withstood the tempests and the floods, and the other house which was built on the sands, which, when the floods came, and the rain descended, and the winds blew and beat upon it, fell; and great was the fall thereof. The fate of those two houses, Jesus said, was a picture of the fate of those who believed His Word and obeyed Him, and those who doubted His Word and rejected Him.

Why is it that this question of doubt arises when we come to the subject of religion, our relationship to God? The subject of doubt is not raised when we talk about a building or a mountain, or a river. The thing is there, manifest and obvious. But when we come to the object of faith, we are in a different field, we are dealing with the intangible, the unseen, and the eternal. Thus the apostle said in that greatest of all definitions of the Christian faith, "Faith is the substance of things hoped for, the evidence of things not seen."

It is at first a rather striking fact that in all the Old Testament, the great New Testament and Christian word "faith" is never mentioned, except in one instance in the Book of Deuteronomy, where it is used in an altogether different meaning. But if the word "faith" is not in the Old Testament, the fact of it is beautifully and grandly there. One of the great examples of faith overcoming doubt, holding on to the substance of things hoped for and standing on the evidence of things not seen, is the story of Elijah after the trial by fire in his great encounter with the prophets of Baal on Mount Carmel. The frenzied prophets of Baal, mocked and taunted by Elijah, had shouted and prayed and cut themselves in vain. No fire came down from heaven to devour their offering. But after Elijah prayed, "Hear me, O Lord, hear me, that this people may know that Thou art the Lord God, and that Thou hast truned their hearts back," the fire fell from heaven and consumed the burnt offering and licked up the water with which Elijah had drenched the altar. When the people saw it they fell on their knees and cried out, "The Lord, He is God!"

Elijah then announced to King Ahab that there would be rain, and that the long drought would be broken. He then told his servant to stand on the top of Mount Carmel and look toward the sea, while he himself went down the mountain a little and, prostrating himself before God, with his face between his knees, prayed for the rain. Standing on the top of Carmel, and looking off toward the Mediterranean, over what is now the considerable city of Haifa, the chief port of the Holy Land, Elijah's servant saw nothing, only the sky like brass and the sea like glass. Not a ripple upon the face of the sea; not the slightest breath of wind, not the slightest whisp of a cloud in the heavens. Then he returned to Elijah and said, "There is nothing." Elijah, still prostrated in prayer, told the young man to go to the top of Carmel again, and again look toward the sea for the sign of rain. Again the young man climbed to the top of the mountain and surveyed the sky and sea, and again he returned to Elijah and said to him, "There is nothing." Elijah sent him up the third time, and a third time he came back and reported, "There is nothing." The prophet sent him back a fourth time, and a fifth time, and a sixth time, and a seventh time. This time the servant came back and said, "Behold, there ariseth a little cloud out of the sea, like a man's hand." In a few minutes the heaven was black with clouds and wind, and there was the sound of the coming of rain. Now Elijah in his triumph girt up his loins and ran before the chariot of Ahab to the palace at Jezreel. It was a great triumph of faith, faith that could wait upon God, faith when everything seems to be against it.

I

DOUBT AS TO GOD

We send out the ambassador of our mind and soul to stand on the highest eminence of human reason and experience and knowledge, and tell us whether or not there is a God. At first, the answer seems to be, "There is nothing." "I cannot hear His voice. I cannot see Him. Behold, I go forward and He is not there, and backward but I cannot behold Him." The very silence of nature oppresses the soul of man in his search for God. In his great hymn which we sing to the grand music of Haydn, Joseph Addison evidently was troubled by that silence, for he said:

> "What though in solemn silence all
> Move round this dark terrestrial ball?
> What though no real voice nor sound
> Amidst the radiant orbs be found?"

That is just the trouble. The solemn silence of it all; and that silence seems to say, "There is nothing."

Yet another look at the world is all on the side of faith and God. Here is the great world, the universe. This mighty effect must have had a correspondingly great cause. And who but God can be that Cause? The world itself, and its order and design, are a mighty argument from common sense for the fact of God. The Scottish poet, James Beattie, who was so overcome by the death of his gifted son that he buried for a time his own poems in that son's grave, afterwards, in a calmer moment, and when the paroxysm of his grief was passed, related how when that son was a child he had given him no instruction as to God or the Christian Faith. But one day, when the child was able to make out letters and read a little, he planted his name with seeds on the garden. After a time, the child came running to his father, and told him his name was growing in the garden. The father at first made light of it, but upon the son's insistence he went out with him to the garden. Beattie looked down at the grass or flowers which spelled the child's name, and said, "That is nothing; it just happened so." "But no," said the boy, "it cannot have just happened so. Someone must have planted it." With that for a start, the father told the boy to look at himself, his eyes, his ears, his tongue, his hands and feet. Could that be just a happen so? And the boy said, No; someone must have made him. A simple, yet profound, illustration of how the world with its order, and man with his fearfully and wonderfully made nature, is a monument to the existence and the power of God.

But now comes perhaps a more serious question. If God is, then what about all the pain, and hardships and suffering that there is in the world. "I am disquieted," the Psalmist said, "when I think upon God." The atheist has no problem of the universe; but a believer has. Here again common sense is on the side of belief. If one should say that pain, and sorrow, and hardships, argue against the existence of God, then it would be equally true that joy, and happiness, and hope, and the zest of living argue *for* the existence of a God. And there is no question that there is more joy and well being in the world than pain and sorrow. Ask any man who has lived fifty or seventy years, whether his body has experienced more hours of pain or more hours of health, and there will be only one answer. Ask anyone who has lived long enough in life to test it by experience, whether he has had more hours of sorrow or more hours of joy, and there is only one answer.

But what about sin and wickedness in the world? What about these massacres and brutal conquests, and cruel "blitzkriegs," the crushing of the helpless and the weak, the enthronement and worship of brute force? Does it not look at first as if either God is not altogether good—could stop sin in the world, but will not, or that He is not altogether powerful—would like to destroy sin in the world, but cannot? In other words, as Friday asked his theological instructor, Robinson Crusoe, when they came up to the subject of the devil, "Why doesn't God kill the devil?" Why does He hid himself so wondrously as if there were no God at all? Why does He seem to be the least seen when all the powers of ill are most abroad?

Here, again, the great arguments of common sense are all on the side of faith. Man is as we know him. God created him free to choose, though also free to fall. So created, not an automation, but a man in the image of God, man chose, and chooses, to sin and to fall. That is the secret of the world's woe and misery, why the whole creation, as Paul put it, groaneth and travaileth in pain until now. But to counteract that disaster, God has set great forces in operation, and that brings us to the next great fact of our faith, the Fact of Christ and His redemption.

II

CHRIST AND SALVATION

Christian faith declares that Jesus, who was born at Bethlehem, who died on the Cross, was the Eternal Son of God. The mind of man wants to know how that could be. How could the Father be God, and Jesus Christ, the Son, also be God? And not only that, but the Holy Ghost, the Comforter, also God? There is the truth, the Trinity, which is the broad foundation of all Christianity. It is the inescapable inference from the teaching of the New Testament and from the teaching of Jesus Christ. But *how* that can be, how the Father is God, how the Son is God, and the Spirit is God, that is one of the things which God hath hid. It is not contrary to man's reason, but above it and beyond it.

The great work of Christ was to redeem man from sin. That He did by His once offering of Himself on the Cross a sacrifice to satisfy Divine Justice. His body was broken, He said, and His blood was spilled for the remission of sins. Just how that can be, just why it is that the agony and death of Christ on the Cross could represent the penalty that is due to man

for His sin, and be a substitute for it; just how it is
that by the same great transcendent, overwhelming
act on the Cross, Christ vindicated the holiness and
justice of God, and at the same time opened the
gates of His mercy—just how it is that by the death
of Christ on the Cross God remained just, yet the
Justifier of them that believe in Jesus—why, even the
angels themselves, we are told, the unfallen and supreme intelligences of Heaven, are curious about that
and "desire to look into it." But as to man's need of
such a redemption, as to the reasonableness of it, the
naturalness of it, yes, we may say, since God is love,
the inevitableness of it—as to that, everything in
man's life and experience and hope is on the side of
the fact of redemption through the love of God and a
Crucified Redeemer.

III

THE LIFE TO COME

Here, of all places, when we send out the ambassador of the soul and mind to report on what happens
to man after death, the answer seems to be, "There
is nothing!" All the facts seem to be against it.
There is hope of a tree, if it be cut down, that it will
live again, and that through the scent of water it will
bud and bring forth. But man lies down, and where
is he? Where do we go from here? We look around
in every direction, and the answer appears to be, Nowhere! There is nothing! Death reigneth! Dead

empires, dead civilizations, dead vegetation; the Universe like a great cemetery; and generation after generation of mankind plunging over the ledge of time into the abyss of eternity. Millions and millions have crossed the border, but none has returned. That world is still

> "The undiscovered country from whose bourne
> No traveler returns."

But that is not all. When we look again, and ask again, we see something more than "nothing." We see a cloud on the horizon of tomorrow no bigger than a man's hand, and yet which points to the great revelation of life eternal in Jesus Christ.

We have the idea of God, and the idea of immortality. One may say that shrewd and cunning priests and impostors invented the idea, so that they might exploit or enslave their fellow man. But if the idea has no corresponding reality, where could they have found it? There is also the universal instinct for immortality, and if God has no organ with which to satisfy that instinct, then His plan is in strange contrast with what we see all about us in this world.

The sense of right and wrong, the sense of justice, the feeling that the Judge of all the earth, must do right, that too, is on the side of future life. Otherwise, we should have to believe that an Ahab or Elijah, a Jesus and a Pilate, a St. Paul and a Nero, fare just the same at death. There is the sense, too, of the incompleteness of our life. Whether it is a life that has lived but for a few days, or a life that lived long, but never found its place, or its platform, or the theater of its expression, or a life that was long and greatly gifted, and richly and nobly served its day and generation, still, at the end there is the sense of incompleteness. It is but a broken column. Something must be added to the story.

Since all this is true, why should it be thought a strange thing that all these intimations of immortality, all those desires for immortality, were at length crowned by the great revelation in Jesus Christ Himself, who said, "I am the Resurrection, and the Life. Whosoever liveth and believeth in Me shall never die"? The great mind of Plato, after recounting all the reasons and all the hopes of a future life, looked forward to such a revelation, for he said that out of all these reasons for a future life we must select that one which seems the strongest, and sail on it as a raft through the stormy seas, until we get something better, such as a revelation. And now that revelation has come! Christ has brought life and immortality to life through the gospel.

I wish I could make you feel, as I feel, what Paul calls "the exceeding greatness of the Christian revelation." I wish I could make you feel, as I feel, how the great arguments from common sense and experience are all on the side of Christian faith, and of a nature to confirm it.

In getting the best of Doubt, there are certain important aids to our faith in this conflict. One of these is humility. Christ laid that down as a condition. "Except ye become as little children, ye shall in no wise enter into the kingdom of Heaven." Another is sincerity of purpose. "If thine eye be single, thy whole body will be full of light." And another is obedience and loyalty to the truth and the light, so far as we have it. This is something that is said over and over again in the Bible, and with many beautiful variants: "Unto the upright there ariseth light in darkness." "Light is sown for the righteous, and gladness for the upright in heart." "We shall know, if we follow on to know the Lord." "If any man will do His will, He shall know of the doctrine, whether it be God, or whether I speak of myself."

One of America's famous preachers, Horace Bushnell, speaking once at Yale College, pointed to a nearby dormitory, and, although in the third person, related how in one of those little rooms he had passed as a student through a great crisis, and had come to a firm faith in God. At that time he could see God but dimly, was not sure that there was a God; and yet he knew that he had a certain sense of duty, and of right; and he knew, too, that he had not always lived up to that sense of duty and of right; and kneeling down he prayed to God that henceforth, although God was but dimly seen, He would make him absolutely faithful and loyal to conscience, to a sense of right. When he rose from his knees he says that it was as if he had wings. Never again did he have doubt as to God, his Maker, and Preserver, and Redeemer.

There is a great prayer offered by St. Paul in his letter to the Romans. At the end of the letter he prays for those Roman Christians, "The God of hope fill you with all joy and peace in believing, that ye may abound in hope, through the Holy Spirit." Joy and Peace in believing! Yes, that is it! Religion, our Christian faith, is not given us to make us uneasy or restless, or troubled, or unhappy. It is not something which we are merely to hold and defend with desperation and with distress. It is designed to give us joy and peace. And only those who believe come to the heights and depths of joy and peace. You remember how our Lord said so frequently to those whom He was about to heal, or who were in any trouble, "Believest thou?" Christ could do none of His gracious works in a certain district "because," say the evangelist, "of their unbelief." But where we believe, there Christ can do great things for you. "Believest thou on the Son of God?"

XIII

GETTING THE BEST OF DEATH

"O Death, where is thy victory?"

I Corinthians 15:55

THAT was the triumphant cry of a man who won the victory over death for himself, and by his own faith and example has helped multitudes of other souls to get the best of Death.

Life is the greatest thing we know, and always in company with life waits death. Ever since Cain, through whose sin death came in the world, looked for the first time upon the face of death and wondered what it was that had made him brotherless, death, the old, old fashion, has been here. The Christian apostle did not overstate it when he referred to the sway of death as the reign of a monarch —"nevertheless, death reigned from Adam to Moses," and, he might have added, from Adam till Christ. James Shirley wrote three hundred years ago,

"The glories of our blood and state
    Are shadows, not substantial things;
There is no armour against fate;
    Death lays his icy hands on kings;
    Scepter and crown
    Must tumble down
And in the dust be equal made
With the poor crooked scythe and spade."

Visiting once a Pennsylvania cemetery where President Buchanan is buried, I saw on a grave this inscription:

> "Leaves have their time to fall,
> And flowers to wither at the North wind's breath,
> And stars to set; but all,
> Thou hast all seasons for thine own, O Death!" [1]

After we have learned the whole vocabulary of life, each one of us at length, at the appointed hour, must learn to pronounce the last and inevitable word, which is Death.

To get the best of Death, then, is indeed a great victory. Yet, it has been done, and by the help of God each one of us can do it.

Let me speak first of how *not* to get the victory over Death. You cannot get the victory over Death by pretending to regard Death lightly, as if it were just an incident of no importance. Still less can you get the victory over Death by denying that there is such a thing, such a fact as Death. The author of the lines was a Christian man, and he said it in the light of Christian faith, at the time of the death of his little daughter. But put in the mouth of an unbeliever, as it so often is, that stanza has no meaning whatever, and is simply a poetic denial of the facts of life.

[1] Felicia Hemans.

GETTING THE BEST OF DEATH

"There is no death! What seems so is transition;
    This life of mortal breath
Is but a suburb of the life elysian,
    Whose portal we call Death!" [2]

Death is not a phantom, not an imagination, not something you can dismiss with a few words of poetry, but a mighty, an inevitable fact, and that is, the separation of the body and the soul. No victory, therefore, will be won over Death by discounting it or shutting our eyes to its significance.

I
NEVER LET DEATH SURPRISE YOU

Now let us speak on the positive side. Prepare for a victory over Death by the determination that Death shall never take you by surprise. Queen Elizabeth once said, "Whatever befalls me, death will never find me unprepared." To a friend who was driving me somewhat more rapidly than I cared to go, I said, "You ought not to think that all others are mortal but yourself." He answered promptly, "I do not so think, for I know that Death rides right here at my side every day." It is an inexcusable blunder for any man to let Death take him by surprise, for Death is the most advertised and the most publicized fact in all human experience. Death has great power. He can lift a king out of his throne; he can sever the closest bond that binds human hearts together; he can over-

[2] Longfellow.

throw the mightiest conqueror. Yet with all these extraordinary powers, Death seems to be the poorest of all preachers, the dullest and most unheeded; for, in spite of the fact that he is forever preaching and daily declaring, "Remember now thy Creator in the days of thy youth," his sermons seem to have less effect upon man's mind and conduct than anything that man hears. Louis XV, King of France, foolishly ordained and ordered that Death was never to be spoken of in his presence. Nothing that could in any way remind him of Death was to be mentioned or displayed, and he sought to avoid every place and sign and monument which in any way suggested Death. Carlyle said of him, "It is the resource of the ostrich, who, hard hunted, sticks his foolish head in the ground and would fain forget that his foolish body is not unseen too." There is no reason why a brave and sensible man should not face all the facts of life, and one of these, and the ultimate fact, so far as this world is concerned, is the fact of Death. Therefore, never let Death take you by surprise.

II

BY PREPARING FOR DEATH

Since Death is inevitable, since "it is appointed unto all men once to die, and after that the judgment," it is wise to make preparation for this final duty and engagement of life.

[166]

One way to do this is by the preparation of a good and honorable and upright life, a life enriched by good deeds. The sting of Death and the victory of the grave are most striking in the death of a man whose life has not been governed by the laws of right and charity and kindness. It is there that Death erects his throne and crowns himself. But in the death of the good man Death inflicts no sting, and the grave has no victory to celebrate.

Wandering once through an Old Testament cemetery, I came upon these two epitaphs, both on the graves of young men, and yet how different in meaning and suggestion and recollection and in hope. One was this:

"He departed without being desired."

The other was this:

"And all Israel mourned over him."

Both were sons of kings, both had great advantages, both lived short lives, but that was the record they left behind them. When one died the whole nation mourned over him. When the other died he departed without being desired. It is when a man has lived the selfish and solitary life and departs without being desired, that death seems garbed in the raiment of a victor.

Once in the beautiful Protestant Cemetery at

Rome, which stands just near the Pyramid of Cestius, hard by where St. Paul was beheaded, not far from the graves of Shelley and Keats, I came suddenly upon the grave of a distinguished Professor of Latin whom I had known in my University days. Not long afterwards, reading a memorial article about him in the *Alumni Magazine*, I came across a sentence from Tacitus which this professor used to quote to his classes—how it was the duty and obligation of every man "to leave behind him a pleasant memory of himself."

In one of his most powerful descriptions of the end of a man's life—and no one described the passing of a good life more beautifully than he did, and none made the passing of an evil life more terrible—Dickens describes the selfish, hard, and unkind man who is compelled by a phantom to contemplate the scenes of his own death, the low people that gather around his body, the plundered bedroom, the vulgar talk. There death sets up his throne: "O cold, cold, rigid, dreadful Death, set up thine altar here and dress it with such terrors as thou hast at thy command; for this is thy dominion! But of the loved, revered, and honored head, thou canst not turn one hair to thy dread purpose, or make one feature odious. It is not that the hand is heavy and will fall down when released; it is not that the heart and pulse are still; but that the hand was open, generous, and true; the heart brave, warm, and tender; and the pulse a man's. Strike, Shadow, strike! And see his good deeds springing from the wound; to sow the world with life immortal."

Those who visit the chapel at Washington and Lee University, where the great Confederate Captain lies buried, are conducted to his study. There everything is just as he left it when he went out of that office for the last time. How are things in the office and study of your life? Is everything just as you would wish to leave it, and leave it never to be changed?

A yet more important preparation for Death and for getting the victory over Death is by repentance and faith in the Lord Jesus Christ. When St. Paul received his summons and knew that the hour of his departure was at hand, he sent his last message to Timothy and to the world. And in that message he said, "I am ready—for I know whom I have believed, and am persuaded that he is able to keep that which I have committed unto him against that day." Paul had a friend, a companion, a guide, and a Saviour who was with him to the last. He did not take that last and hardest stretch of life's journey alone.

On November 20, 1847, there died at Nice, France, Henry Frances Lyte, a retired and long-time ill Church of England curate, who had worn himself out in charitable labors in the slums of London. At his death his family found the almost illegible manuscript of a poem he had written during those last days, now a hymn which has sung itself around the world. It was this:

> "Abide with me: fast falls the eventide;
> The darkness deepens; Lord, with me abide!
> When other helpers fail, and comforts flee,
> Help of the helpless, O abide with me."

There was a man whose faith in Christ enabled him to get the best of Death, and the hymn which he left behind him has helped multitudes of other souls to gain that great victory.

The hour of death is appointed. It is written in God's book. We need not concern ourselves about that. Our duty is to live the right life and to put our faith now in Christ. After the battle of Bull Run, Imboden asked Stonewall Jackson, who had received a painful wound in the battle, "General, how is it that you can keep so cool and appear so utterly insensible to danger in such a storm of shell and bullets as rained about you when your hand was hit?" "Captain," answered Jackson in a grave and reverential manner, "my religious belief teaches me to feel as safe in battle as in bed. God has fixed the time for my death. I do not concern myself about that, but to be always ready no matter when it may overtake me." Then, after a pause, he added, "That is the way all men should live, and then all would be equally brave."

III

VICTORY OVER DEATH IN THE LIVES OF OTHERS

So far, we have spoken of our own relationship to Death, and how to get the best of Death in our own lives. But there is another and very important aspect of this subject, and that is how to get the best of Death in the lives of others. By this I mean that a great many are overcome by Death and sadly influenced by the effect of Death in the lives of others. Perhaps Death does as much damage to human lives in this way as directly—that is, by the shadow that it casts upon the lives of the living. Thus it gains dominion over multitudes of souls, paralyzing their energies, withering their joy, and clouding their hope. It is easy enough to sink into this kind of defeat in the time of bereavement and sorrow; but victory always requires an effort. How then can we get the best of Death in the lives of our friends?

We can get the best of Death in other lives by the recollection of what was good and worthy in them. That is a sure and abiding inheritance, if we will have it so. The recollection of their lives can inspire us to live more nobly. Indeed, how could some of us keep steady and true and faithful and believing, were it not for the recollection of friends who have passed into Immanuel's Land?

Another way to get the best of Death in the lives

of others is to permit such sorrow to discipline and enlarge us. It ought to make us realize anew the brevity of life, and that we must work while it is called today ere the night cometh when no man can work. Let me then sing my best song, do my best work, write the best page I can, preach the best sermon I can, show the best example I can, for the day is short, and tomorrow my opportunity may be gone.

In a yet more definite Christian sense we can get the best of Death in the lives of others by the exercise of Christian faith, by the belief, grounded upon the great assurances and the great acts of our Saviour Jesus Christ, that the souls of the righteous are in the hands of God. They have been parted from us for a season that we might have them forever. In this world we have had their example, their friendship, their companionship. Now we have their memory, the companionship of their spirits, and in the future, their fellowship at God's right hand, where there are pleasures forevermore.

Azrael, according to tradition, was the Angel of Death. There is a beautiful thought concerning Azrael, that the reason he casts such a shadow upon the soul in this world is that, although his feet are planted on the earth, his head is in heaven, aureoled with the splendor of God's light. That is why he casts a shadow over men when he stoops from the unfathomed height of heaven to lift to God those whom we call dead.

> "Angel of Death, who like some monstrous cloud
>   Blotting the sun and drenching earth in gloom,
>   With dreadful wings outspread, of raven plume,
> God and His Heaven from our eyes dost shroud
> In night impenetrable—art thou proud
>   Of thy poor triumph in man's hopeless doom,
>   Of thy fell incense from the fetid tomb,
> Thy hymns of ceaseless lamentation loud?—
> Or is it that we cannot see aright?
>   Hast thou thy feet on earth, in Heaven thy head,
> Aureoled with splendor of God's living light?
>   Isn't that which casts on us thy shadow dread,
> When thou dost stoop from that unfathomed height
>   To lift to God those whom we call the dead?" [3]

May God grant us all that great victory of which Paul spake when he said, "Thanks be unto God who giveth us the victory through our Lord and Saviour Jesus Christ." May we all live in such close and trusting and loving relationship to our Lord and Redeemer that we can say, "I am persuaded that neither death, nor life, nor angels, nor principalities, nor powers, nor things present, nor things to come, shall be able to separate us from the love of God, which is in Christ Jesus our Lord."

[3] Herbert H. Yeames, in *Catholic World.*

XIV

GETTING THE BEST OF MYSELF
"Ye shall win your souls"
Luke 21:19

ONCE in his dream a man was haunted and thwarted by a mysterious veiled figure. As soon as he had gained a fortune, the veiled form snatched it away from him. When he was about to enter into peace and joy, the veiled figure attacked his mind with fear and anxiety. When he was hungry and sat down to eat, the veiled figure snatched his food away from him. When he was overcome with slumber and lay down to sleep, this enemy of his life filled his mind with thoughts which banished sleep. When he had won fame, the veiled figure took away his reputation. When he stood at the open door of a great opportunity and was about to enter, the hand of the veiled one suddenly closed the door against him. When he stood at last at the marriage altar, and was about to give his sacred avowal and take the hand of his bride in wedlock, the veiled one strode forth, and, lifting up his hand in protest, said, "I forbid the banns!" Enraged, the unhappy man cried out to his adversary, "Who art thou?" and, stretching forth his hand, seized the veil and ripped it from the face of the tormentor, and lo, the face that he saw was his own!

This dream sets forth the great truth that man is his own chief adversary and foe. If he is his own best friend, he is also his own worst enemy. Men make or ruin themselves. Our fault is not in our stars, but in ourselves, and we are the ones, and the only ones, who make or mar our destiny.

In this series of sermons which now comes to a close, we have spoken of certain of the adversaries of man's life, things which stand between him and happiness, and strength, and influence. There are many more adversaries than the fourteen which we have named and upon which we have spoken, but there is no doubt that these fourteen adversaries, such as Fear, with which we commenced, and the Past, Sex and Love, our Enemies, Jealousy, Anger, the Tongue, and Doubt, are real foes of our life. But all of these enemies lodge in our own souls. In their warfare against us they use ourselves as a base of operation. They attack us through ourselves; hence, in the last analysis, the victory of life, "How to Face Life and Get the Best of It," is a question of how to get the victory over our own souls.

When He had told them in advance of some of the difficulties and trials and sufferings which would beset them, Christ said to His disciples: "By your steadfastness ye shall win your souls." This "winning of our souls," this victory over ourselves, is the greatest possession and the greatest conquest of all. There is no city, no kingdom, so rich as the kingdom of your own soul. The ancient world made the taking of a city the greatest of all human achievements. The page of history abounds in the accounts of the conquests of great cities, and how, either by process of slow siege, or by sudden assault, the invading army stormed the walls and entered the city, leaving death and devastation in its trail. Then, on an appointed day, the conqueror, mounted on his war charger, or standing in his gilded chariot, made a triumphal entry into the city. Through broken-down walls he drove, to pass in triumph along the streets and avenues, flanked by profaned temples and smoking homes; and as he passed, the cheers of the conquerors had a dismal antiphony in the groans of the vanquished. This was what it meant to take a city. It was the utmost of human achievement, the most renowned and most distinguished of the exploits of man. But even at that remote age, when the conqueror of a city or a nation was still the greatest figure on the human horizon, there were those who saw that there was a still greater conquest and victory—the Conquest of Self. The greatest and most imperial city of all is the city of the human soul, whose walls and turrets, whose gates and towers, are to be found beneath every human breast. He who takes that city and rules it in the interests of reason and faith is the King of all conquerors. So it was written by one of the greatest kings and rulers the world has ever seen, "He that ruleth his own spirit is greater than he that taketh a city."

The chief foe and adversary of life is our own self. A great preacher, and a great winner of souls too, said: "I have had more trouble with myself than with any other person I ever knew." Very often men are reluctant to admit this. They like to blame the stars, outside circumstances, other people, for their difficulties and hardships, or lack of success in life. But now and then you hear a striking confession which confirms the truth with which we are dealing, that man is the architect of his own destiny. I once asked a husbandless mother, who had come to plan for her child, how she managed to get into this difficult circumstance, for if she told me, I said to her, on the ground of her experience I might be able to help someone else. Her answer was brief and to the point: "I have no one to blame but myself." On another occasion, visiting one of our great penal institutions, as I went from one inmate to another, I began to say to myself, All these people here seem to have the idea that they are not to blame for their circumstances. Nearly all tried to give me the impression that they were innocent of wrongdoing, and were the victims of injustice or circumstances. But in talking with one man I asked him, in a kindly way, what his trouble was. He answered at once, "No trouble, sir, but myself."

How often that phrase, that sentence, has echoed in my memory: "No trouble, sir, but myself." The deepest and most dangerous troubles which afflict man's life come from within, not from without. Man's soul, that great fortress of Bunyan's imagination, fell only when there was treason within. The enemy entered through a gate that had been opened from within. The outside dangers and temptations of the world have no power over us *until* they receive the co-operation and help of the foe within our own souls.

If our chief foe is within our own souls, so also is our chief ally and friend. The German poet Goethe used to have a saying, "Here, or nowhere, is thine America." What he meant was that there were many people who hoped to get the highest blessing out of life by migrating to America. But no change of the physical surroundings of life could bring them the blessing and happiness of life. That depends upon the man himself. "Here, or nowhere, is thine America."

When the prophet of Israel gave King Ahab instruction and encouragement for the coming battle with the hosts of Syria, and how a great victory would be won by Israel, the king said to him, "Who

shall command the battle?" And he said unto him,
"Thou!" And that is forever true. In this battle
against Fear, this battle with the appetites of the
body, this battle with Anger, this battle with Jealousy, this battle with the Past, this battle with Doubt
—in short, this whole campaign and warfare with
self—there is only one man who can command the
battle, and that man is Thyself. Thou art the man!
Others can advise you, counsel you, warn you, pray
for you, hope for you; but in the battle you are the
sole commander; if you lose, the sole loser, and if you
win, the sole conqueror.

Sir Edwin Arnold, author of *The Light of Asia,*
speaking once to the students at Harvard College,
said: "In 1776 you conquered your fathers (referring
to the war of the Revolution). In 1861 you conquered your brothers. Now the next great victory is
to conquer yourselves." That is true of America as
a nation. But in a particular sense it is true of us as
individuals. We must conquer ourselves.

Nearly all the tragedies of life are the tragedies
of battles where man has been betrayed and overcome
by his own soul. We must believe that there is a
nobler self within us, a self that we must set free and
crown. In one of his tales Dickens, describing a low,
coarse woman, says of her that, after going through
many narrow passages, and up winding stairs, and
down narrow hallways, you come at last to a door

upon which is written the word, "Woman." What he meant to say was that even in the lowest and worst of women there was something that is noble and womanly. So within every life there is the capacity of greatness. Underneath every covering of the rubbish and sin and defilement of life, you come at length upon a door on which is engraved that most wonderful of words, The Soul—that soul that is yours by virtue of your creation in the Divine Image, that soul that sin has marred and defiled and fettered and choked, but could never destroy, that soul for the redemption of which Christ shed His precious blood on Calvary's Tree.

In the battle for the soul, to win and possess this great trophy, we must expect hardship, and pain, and denial, and suffering. That was what Christ meant when He said, "By your patience (or better, literally, by your steadfastness, your endurance) ye shall win your souls." When we have the sense of the value of the soul, of what is at stake, then we can endure loss and hardship in its behalf. The higher thought conquers the lesser consideration. When the thirty-two British sailors who had been taken from merchant ships lay locked in their iron cells in the brig of the ship, down in the bowels of the German battleship the Graf Spee, during that running battle recently off the coast of Uruguay, they cheered every time they heard a shell from the British cruisers strike the sides

[181]

of the German ship. They knew that a British victory, a British shell going through the Graf Spee might well mean the destruction of their own lives; yet they cheered, because the higher thought, the thought of country, the thought of the cause of Democracy and freedom in the world, had conquered the lower thought, the thought of their own danger, or their own deliverance from death. Thus it is that the high thought, and the consideration of what is most sacred in life, arms us to endure and to conquer.

In the battle for the soul we do not fight alone. The old medieval legends sometimes tell of great knights and warriors who had the strength of a hundred men and could overcome all their enemies against tremendous odds, because they had a secret or an invisible captain who fought by their side, or gave strength to their blows. In this battle for the possession of our souls, we have the presence and help of the Captain of our Salvation. The Scotch poet Henley once wrote in memory of Hamilton Bruce those ringing and oft-quoted stanzas, "Invictus":

> "Out of the night that covers me
>   Black as the pit from pole to pole,
> I thank whatever gods there be
>   For my unconquerable soul.
>
> In the fell clutch of circumstance
>   I have not winced nor cried aloud;
> Under the bludgeonings of chance
>   My head is bloody, but unbowed.

Beyond this place of wrath and tears
　Looms but the horror of the shade;
And yet the menace of the years
　Finds, and shall find me, unafraid.

It matters not how strait the gate,
　How charged with punishments the scroll,
I am the master of my fate;
　I am the captain of my soul."

Whatever Henley meant by those thoroughly pagan lines, this is not what the Christian means when he speaks of self-conquest. It was not what Paul meant when he said that Christ was the Captain of his soul. The man who wrote the paraphrase of Henley's ringing lines struck the note and the secret of Christian self-control when he said:

"Out of the light that dazzles me,
　Bright as the sun from pole to pole,
I thank the God I know to be
　For Christ, the Conqueror of my soul.

Since His the sway of circumstance,
　I would not wince, nor cry aloud;
Under that Rule, which men call chance,
　My head with joy is humbly bowed.

Beyond this place of sin and tears,
　That life with Him—and His the aid,
That, spite the menace of the years,
　Keeps, and will keep, me unafraid.

[185]

"I have no fear, though strait the gate;
   He cleared from punishment the scroll;
Christ is the Master of my fate!
   Christ is the Captain of my soul." [1]

Who, then, shall be the captain of thy soul—
thyself or Christ?

[1] Author unknown.